Award Winning Architecture
International Yearbook 96

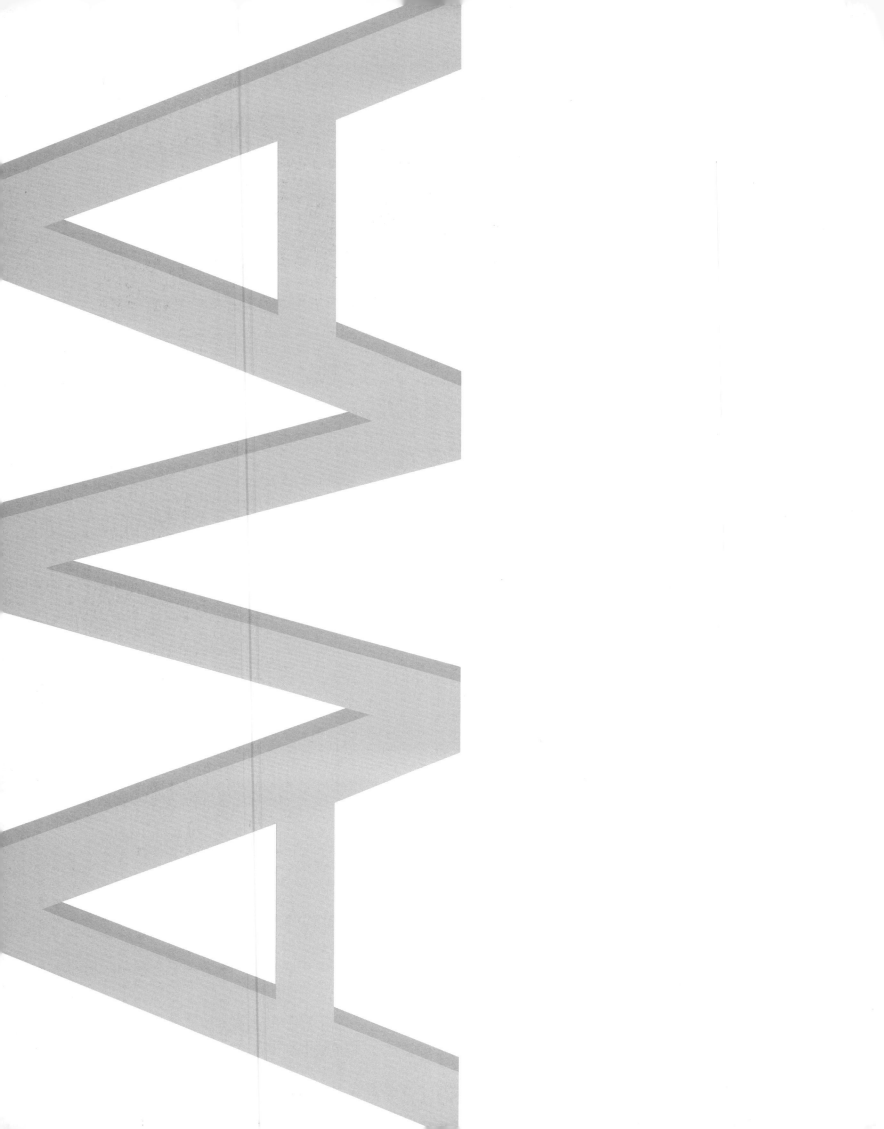

Award Winning Architecture
AWA 96

Edited by
Frantisek Sedlacek

in cooperation with
Christine Waiblinger-Jens

Patron
UIA (International Union of Architects)

Prestel Munich · New York

Contents

**COMPREHENSIVE LISTING OF PROJECTS:
AWARD WINNING ARCHITECTURE 1996**

DETAILED DESCRIPTIONS OF SELECTED PROJECTS:
A REPRESENTATIVE CROSS-SECTION

Finis coronat opus

We live and move in buildings that influence the way we act and think.
The quality of the architecture affects the way we perceive a building.

What, objectively speaking, is architectural quality?

Building is an ancient human activity that springs from two very different sources.
On the one hand, people throughout the ages have built in order to provide shelter from
the elements, while on the other hand, creative freedom has always given each building
its distinctive character.
A building has to fulfil certain pragmatic requirements which determine the sphere
within which the architect's imagination can operate.
Neither reason nor emotion alone are enough in the creation of a building or in the
creation of architecture as such.
Spatial visions are controlled by the mind. Or, to put it more simply: first they are right,
and then they are beautiful.

›The art of architecture‹ is perceptual and relational.
Information conveyed by architecture must necessarily be aesthetic. In other words, in
the original Greek sense of the term, it must be perceptible to the senses.
The tangible, palpable, visible, object-related specificity of our built and designed
environment dictates the limits of our experience for aesthetic perception.
The unity of content, construction and design – in other words, perfection of form – is
perceived as beauty.
Beauty as ›freedom‹, art as the ultimate form of individual expression. Beauty and art as
aesthetics or perception.
Moreover, architecture is inextricably linked with the place that makes each building a
unique and unrepeatable entity.

It is not the object alone, but the way it relates to its environmental context, that constitutes
the most important element of architecture.

Between the building and the environment, a mutual relationship of give and take is created.
Genius loci. Both architecture and the environment need this relationship as a means of
reciprocal identification.
What is more, each and every building is, above all, a functional space.
Which is why it has more functional forms than free forms.

Within this extremely limited field, two fundamental tendencies interact.
The progressive, the forward-looking and the experimental arouse more interest than the
sophisticated and the perfect.

Perfection provokes progression towards a communicative opposite.
In time, classical perfection culminates in its own mannerism and futurist progression
mutuates towards new perfection.
A perpetuum of mobile architectural trends and tendencies. A theoretical orientation
that was, is, and will remain valid for all eras, generations and stylistic directions.
From modernism as an expression of the whole, to the additive eclecticism of
postmodernism and on to the individual modernism of today – hi tech, deconstructivism,
purism or rationalism – architecture, like the entire spectrum of our culture and civilisation,
is moving towards the future.
Towards a future we do not know. Quo vadis architecture?

I am not an architecture theorist. I am not an architecture critic. I am an architect.
I regard the art of building as an expression of society. Throughout the world, people live
in very different social forms. With their own values and aims, ideas and prospects. Under
different political, cultural, technical and economic conditions.
Needless to say, this leads to different notions of what constitutes good architecture.
Buildings generally acknowledged as being of particular value document this eloquently.
In the flood of information, we seek reliability. We seek to support or relativise subjective
evaluations by means of objective decisions.
A jury's decision to award a prize to a building should guarantee an objective evaluation of
architectural quality. If that jury is made up only of architects, the highest possible degree
of objectivity ought to be expected.
A book about architecture officially granted an award by architects should therefore
constitute an almost ideal yardstick for contemporary architecture and documents the
specific quality of specific architecture within a specific period.
A body of evidence.

Frantisek D. Sedlacek

Notes on the concept behind this yearbook

AWA – Award Winning Architecture – International Yearbook: for us, the title is at once an inspiration and a commitment. The aim of publishing a yearbook to present completed architectural schemes which have received awards from national associations of architects from all over the world was an exciting challenge, and one we were happy to rise to.

From Algeria to Zimbabwe, architects have formed national associations which, in turn, operate under the auspices of the umbrella organisation UIA (International Union of Architects). Apart from safeguarding the rights and duties of architects, these institutes endeavour to set standards of quality in the built environment and to convey this to the public.
The associations, represented by a jury elected from their ranks, traditionally present awards for the best buildings. Unlike awards presented by industry or the private sector which frequently reflect one-sided interests, the prizes awarded by architects to architects are based on evaluation criteria that ensure a maximum of objectivity.

The reason why an annual synopsis of these awards has not been published to date – given the enormous range of architectural publications available – has become clear to us in the course of the two years spent preparing this publication.
Even the task of finding out the addresses of the respective associations and the names of the appropriate contacts within each organisation required more patience and perseverence than we expected. Often, several different prizes are awarded by a single association, while other associations present awards only at irregular intervals – sometimes years apart.
The idea of a fully comprehensive survey and ›quantitative justice‹ had to be abandoned. After initial contacts had been made with the architects´ associations in some 100 countries, the award winners themselves also had to be contacted with requests for material and information for the planned publication.

Enormous flexibilty was needed shortly before going into print when an unexpected flood of documents arrived, exceeding the bounds of the original publishing concept. Having worked on the premise that we would be presenting about fifty buildings, we suddenly found ourselves confronted with more than 150.
In order to present the buildings as ›democratically‹ as possible, they have been put in alphabetical order according to countries and, within each country, alphabetically according to architects. We have dispensed with any descriptive texts, preferring instead to present plans and photos that speak for themselves. Not all the projects, however, could be illustrated. In such cases, we have provided a brief list of the awards, juries, co-workers and technical data pertaining to the building, as far as these were available.

A selection of forty outstanding projects are presented in detail in a separate section of the book. On the one hand, these works are intended to document international trends in architecture, including developments in countries with comparatively limited financial possibilities. On the other hand, it cannot be denied that in ›architecturally highly ›developed‹ countries more prizes are awarded and that this alone could lead to an imbalance. We have endeavoured to find a ›democratic mean‹ in this section of the book as well. We felt that not only the buildings of internationally renowned architects were of interest, but also, and even especialy, the contributions by young architects and by those who are barely known beyond the borders of their home countries.

This, the first AWA yearbook, includes some buildings already completed a number of years ago but which have only recently received awards. Given the years of preparation involved and the fact that prizes are not awarded annually in all countries, we have also included a number of projects which received awards in the early nineties.

Without exception, all the associations and architects responded very positively to our publishing project and this fact is reflected in the number of contributions received. Moreover, the fact that the UIA has granted its patronage to this project is not only a further confirmation, but also a great honour.

Each and every person whose name is mentioned in any capacity whatsoever on the following pages has made an inestimable contribution to the realisation of this publication. We wish to thank them all for their assistance and cooperation and regret that that we could not present all the buildings in as much detail as we had originally planned. We are pleased to have found a solution which presents a broad spectrum of architecture, combining concise information with high aesthetic standards.

We welcome suggestions and ideas for the AWA yearbook 1997.

Christine Waiblinger-Jens

AWA Award Winning Architecture
Dürener Strasse 260
D - 50935 Köln
Germany

COMPREHENSIVE LISTING OF PROJECTS:
AWARD WINNING ARCHITECTURE 1996

 **Award Winning Architecture** *includes awards from national associations of architects who are members of the UIA, listed country by country in alphabetical order. Within each country, the individual architects are also listed alphabetically. A number of selected projects are documented in detail in the second section of the book, and these are only briefly outlined in the general section, with a cross reference specifying the page on which the detailed description can be found.*

The awards in question are the highest accolades presented by the respective national architects' associations. Where such an association does not actually grant an award itself, an equivalent award by another institution or foundation has been included on the recommendation of the national architects' association.

A

Award Robin Boyd Award for Housing

Architect **Bud Brannigan, St. Lucia**

Award Winning Building **Brannigan Residence**

Page 64

Australia

Award International Citation

Given by The Royal Australian Institute of Architects

Prize Presentation 1994

Architects **Conybeare Morrison & Partners (Australia) and United Consultants (Malaysia)**

Award Winning Building **Kuching Waterfront Development**

Location Kuching, Malaysia

Australia

Award Commercial Architecture Award

Given by The Royal Australian Institute of Architects

Prize Presentation 1994

Architect **Denton Corker Marshall Pty. Ltd.**

Award Winning Building **Governor Phillip Tower (NSW)**

Australia

Award Commercial Architecture Award

Architects **Guymer Bailey Architects Pty. Ltd., Fortitude Valley**

Award Winning Building **Kingfisher Bay Resort and Village (Qld)**

Page 68

Australia

Award International Award

Architects **Kerry Hill Architects (with Akitek Jururancang), Singapore**

Award Winning Building **The Datai (Malaysia)**

Page 72

Australia

Award Environment Citation

Given by The Royal Australian Institute of Architects

Prize Presentation 1994

Architect **Jackson Teece Chesterman Willis**

Award Winning Building **Advanced Technology Centre (NSW)**

Australia

Award National Interiors Architecture Award

Given by The Royal Australian Institute of Architects

Prize Presentation 1994

Members of the Jury Graham Bligh, Peter Crone, Rebecca Gilling, Neville Quarry, James Taylor

Architects **Mitchell / Giurgola & Thorp Architects, New York / Sydney**

Awarded Interior **Allen Allen & Hemsley Offices, Sydney**

Location Chifley Tower, 2 Chifley Square, Sydney, Australia

Design and Construction Period June 1990 - May 1993

Design Team Mitchell / Giurgola & Thorp Architects; Harold S. Guida (Design partner); Richard G. Thorp (Administrative partner); Richard Francis-Jones (Project architect);David Conley, Jeff Morehen, Peter Clarke, Jane Davie, Burt Greer, Sarah Hill, David Ostinga, Jonathan Redman, Scott Lester (Project team)

Structural, Mechanical, Electrical, Lighting Engineering Flack & Kurtz Australia

Project Managing, Quantity Surveying Leighton Contractors Pty Ltd

Total Floor Area 15,000 m²

Photography John Gollings, Sharrin Rees

Australia

Award Sir Zelman Cowen Award for Public Buildings

Given by The Royal Australian Institute of Architects

Prize Presentation 1994

Architects **Glenn Murcutt & Associates Pty. Ltd. and Troppo Architects Pty. Ltd. (Architects in association)**

Australia

Award Winning Building **Bowali Visitor Centre and Headquarters**

Location Kakadu National Park, Australia

13

Award Lachlan Macquarie Award for Conservation

Given by Royal Australian Institute of Architects

Prize Presentation 1994

Members of the jury James Taylor, Graham Bligh, Peter Crone, Rebecca Gilling, Neville Quarry

Architects **Peddle Thorp Architects with Allom Lovell & Associates, Conservation Architects, Melbourne**

Award Winning Building **ANZ Headquarters - Gothic Bank**

Location 380 Collins Street, Melbourne, Australia

Design and Construction Period 1990 -1993 (33 months)

Structural and Civil Engineering Connell Wagner

Quantity Surveying WT Partnership

Mechanical and Electrical Engineering Norman Disney & Young

Interior Design Peddle Thorp Architects with Allom Lovell & Associates, Conservation Architects

Approximate Cost Aus$ 20,000,000

Site Area 397 m²

Building Area 397 m²

Total Floor Area 10,640 m²

Photography Allom Lovell & Associates

Australia

Award Access Citation

Given by The Royal Australian Institute of Architects

Prize Presentation 1994

Australia

Architects **SACON Pty. Ltd.**

Award Winning Building **SA Aquatic Sciences Centre**

Award 1- Walter Burley Griffin Award for Urban Design (National Award) / 2- Victorian Architecture Medal / 3- Merit Award for Outstanding Architecture - Multiple Residential Category

Given by 1- Royal Australian Institute of Architects (National); 2- / 3- Royal Australian Institute of Architects (Victorian Chapter)

Prize Presentation 1- November / 23 /1994; 2- / 3- July 1994

Members of the Jury 1- Neville Quarry, Rebecca Gilling, Peter Crone, James Taylor, Graham Bligh; 2- John Denton, Peter Crone, Peter Sanders, Helen Rice, Steven Whitford, Michael Jeffreson, Tim Hubbard, Dimity Reed; 3- Peter Sanders, Noel McKernan, Robert Harwood, Leo de Jong

Architects **Williams & Boag Pty. Ltd. Architects, Melbourne**

Award Winning Building **Tyne Street Redevelopment**

Location Tyne Street and Little Elgin Street, Carlton

Design and Construction Period March 1991 - June 1994

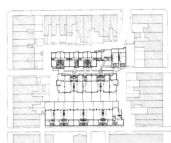

Design Team Peter Williams, Tim Lang, John Clark, Kim Irons, Beth Mell, Richard Marendaz

Structural and Civil Engineering Irwin Johnston & Partners

Quantity Surveying Cost Control / Financial Management by the Project Developer

Mechanical and Electrical Engineering mechanical: Air Systems Engineering ; electrical: Elecraft P/ L Electrical Contractors

Landscape Architecture Mark McWha Landscape Architecture

Approximate Cost Aus$ 7,600,000

Site Area 2,475 m^2

14

Building Area 1,634 m^2

Total Floor Area 5,328 m^2

Photography Trevor Mein, Valeriu Campan, Milan Roden

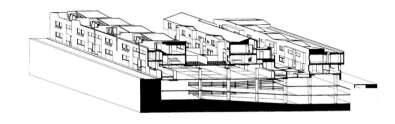

Australia _____

Award 1- Merit Award for Civic Design / 2- Walter Burley Griffin Award for Urban Design

Given by 1- The Royal Australian Institute of Architects, NSW Chapter; 2- RAIA (National)

Prize Presentation 1- June / 30 /1994; 2- November / 23 /1994

Members of the Jury Alex Tzannes, James Taylor

Architect **Tonkin Zulaikha Hartford Architects, Sydney**

Award Winning Building **The Rocks Square - Argyle and Playfair Streets, Sydney**

Location Sydney, Australia

Design and Construction Period 18 months

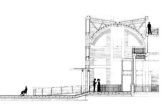

Design Team Tonkin Zulaikha - Peter Tonkin (Director in charge), Andrew Nimmo (Project architect)

Structural Engineering Paterson Wholohan Grill

Services Engineering Engineering Consultants Australia

Quantity Surveying Nelson Brandtman and Partners

Retail Consulting Trading Places

Approximate Cost Aus$ 5,000,000

Site Area 1,940 m^2 (level 1 retail: 820 m^2; level 2 retail: 750 m^2; mezzanine retail: 80 m^2; level 3 + 4 residential: 320 m^2)

Photography Liz Cotter, Assassi

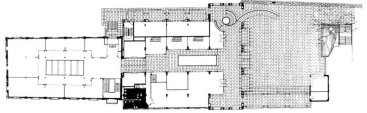

Australia _____

Award Nominierung zum Staatspreis für Consulting

Given by Bundeskammer der Architekten und Ingenieurkonsulenten

Prize Presentation December /1/1994

Members of the Jury Meixner, Purr, Werner, Rant

Austria _____

Architects **Hermann & Valentiny, Architectes, Vienna**

Award Winning Building **Housing Complex, Dessau**

Location Dessau - Ziebigk, Germany

Landscape Architecture Hermann & Valentiny

Award Preis der Zentralvereinigung der Architekten Österreichs

Architects **THE OFFICE, Vienna**

Award Winning Building **Supermarket Merkur**

Austria _____

Page 76

Award Nominierung zum Staatspreis für Consulting - Bereich Revitalisierung

Given by Bundesministerium für Wirtschaftliche Angelegenheiten und Bundeskammer der Architekten und Ingenieurkonsulenten

Prize Presentation Jury: December 1994, Announcement: January 1995

Architects **Christa Prantl, Alexander Runser, Oskar Graf, Vienna**

Award Winning Building **Ehemalige Lanzendorfer Mühle (rebuilding)**

Location Mistelbach, Austria

Design and Construction Period 1990 - 1993

Design Team Christa Prantl, Alexander Runser, Vienna

Structural and Civil Engineering Oskar Graf, Vienna

Interior Design Christa Prantl, Alexander Runser

Approximate Cost ÖS 5,000,000

Site Area 2,015 m²

Building Area 530 m²

Total Floor Area approx. 1,500 m²

Photography Margherita Spiluttini, Vienna

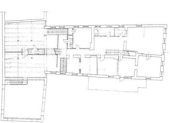

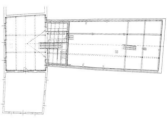

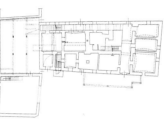

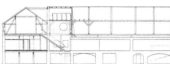

Austria _____

Award Staatspreis für Consulting

Given by Bundeskammer der Architekten und Ingenieurkonsulenten

Prize Presentation 1994

Austria _____

Architect **Scharoplan**

Award Winning Building **Biogenic district heating**

Location Unterneukirchen, Austria

B

Award IAB Gold Medal

Given by The Institute of Architects Bangladesh

Prize Presentation 1994

Bangladesh _____

Architect **Muzharsul Islam**

Award Winning Building **All projects**

15

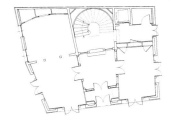

Award Prix Européen de la Reconstruction de la Ville

Given by Fondation Philippe Rotthier pour l'Architecture, Brussels

Prize Presentation October / 21 / 1995

Members of the Jury Maurice Culot, Léon Krier, Demetri Porphyrios, Anxon Martinez Salazar, Gabriele Tagliaventi, Sergio Frau

Architects **Michel Authié et Pierre Sicard**

Award Winning Building **Maison du Tourisme et de la Montagne à Cauterets**

Location Cauterets, Centre Ville, France

Design and Construction Period 12 months

Structural and Civil Engineering BEI PEI

Mechanical and Electrical Engineering Bet Otce

Approximate Cost FF 6,000,000

Site Area 136 m²

Building Area 820 m²

Total Floor Area 136 m²

Photography Michel Authié et Pierre Sicard

Belgium ———————————————————————————

Award Prix Européen de la Reconstruction de la Ville - Category: Espace Public et Projet Urbain

Given by Fondation Philippe Rotthier pour l'Architecture, Brussels

Prize Presentation October / 21 / 1995

Architects **Jacques Leccia and Christian Parra**

Award Winning Building **Le Centre Historique de Bayonne**

Location Bayonne, France

Belgium ———————————————————————————

Award Prix Européen de la Reconstruction de la Ville

Given by Fondation Philippe Rotthier pour l'Architecture, Brussels

Prize Presentation June / 10 / 1995

Members of the Jury Maurice Culot, Léon Krier, Demetri Porphyrios, Anxton Martinez Salazar, Gabriele Tagliaventi and Sergio Frau

Architect **Daniel Staelens, Brussels**

Award Winning Building **Village School, Scariga**

Location Judet of Bacau, Romania

Design and Construction Period February - August 1992

Approximate Cost ECU (all inclusive) 35,000

Site Area 2,000 m²

Building Area 256 m²

Photography Marina Cox, Brussels

Belgium ———————————————————————————

Award Prêmio Habitação / Premiação IAB

Architect **Carlos Bratke, São Paulo**

Award Winning Building **Mountain House**

Page 80

Brazil ———————————————————————————

Award Annual Award of the Instituto de Arquitetos do Brasil -
Departamento de São Paulo - one-person residence
Given by Instituto de Arquitetos do Brasil - Departamento de São Paulo
Prize Presentation March / 22 / 1995
Members of the Jury Joaquim Guedes, Marília Santana de Almeida,
Abrahão Sanovicz, Tito Lívio Frascino, Decio Tozzi, Willis Myasaka,
Gianfranco Vannucchi
Architect **Hélio Hirao, São Paulo**
Award Winning Building **Architect's house**
Location Presidente Prudente, Estado de São Paulo, Brazil
Design and Construction Period design: October 1992 - January 1993,
construction: February 1993 - February 1994

Structural and Civil Engineering Alfredo J. Penha,
Donizetti de Angelo Foster
Quantity Surveying Hélio Hirao
Mechanical and Electrical Engineering Hugo C. Matioli Melo
Landscape Architecture Hélio Hirao
Approximate Cost US$ 30,000
Site Area 360 m²
Building Area 100 m², Area to be built 100 m²
Photography Hélio Hirao

Brazil

17

Award 1- Premiação Instituto de Arquitetos do Brasil / 2- Premio Fachada
(Best Facade)
Given by 1- Insituto de Arquitetos do Brasil; 2- Creativity Club of São Paulo
Prize Presentation 1994
Members of the Jury 1- Abrahão Sanovicz, Gianfranco Vannucchi,
Willis Myasaka, Decio Tozzi, Marilia Santana de Almeida, Tito Livio Frascino;
2- José Eduardo Tibiriçá, Gianfranco Vannucchi, Henrique Cambiaghi,
Marcel Monacelli, Rogério Batagliesi, Edison Musa, Guto Lacas,
José Zaragoza, Caio Túlio Costa
Architect **Marcio Kogan, São Paulo**
Award Winning Building **Larmod (Fabric) Showroom**
Location São Paulo, Brazil
Design and Construction Period January - December 1994

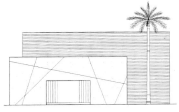

Design Team Marcio Kogan, Oswaldo Pessano, Yara Santucci, Maria
Fernanda Martini
Structural and Civil Engineering Henrique Rosenhek, Furuta Kawasaki,
Mauro Weichemberg
Mechanical and Electrical Engineering Autoraf Prodart: Icaro Machado
Hueza, Ricardo do Nascimento
Interior Design Marcio Kogan, Attilio Baschera, Gregório Kramer
Approximate Cost US$ 700,000
Site Area 750 m²
Building Area 800 m²
Total Floor Area 550 m²
Photography Tuca Reinés

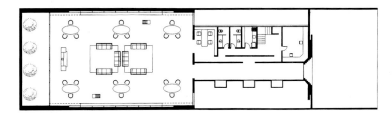

Brazil

Award Premiação IAB-SP 94 - Best Building

Given by Instituto de Arquitetos do Brasil - SP

Prize Presentation March 1995

Members of the Jury Architects: Joaquim Guedes, Marília Santana de Almeida, Abrahão Sanovicz, Tito Lívio, Willis Myasaka, Gianfranco Vanucchi, Decio Tozzi

Architect **Samuel Kruchin, São Paulo**

Award Winning Building **EEPG. Barão de Monte Santo**

Location Mocóca, São Paulo, Brazil

Design and Construction Period 1992 -1995

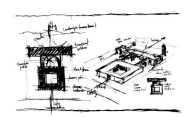
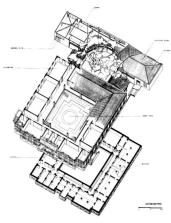

Historical Research Silvia Wolf[2]

Design Team Samuel Kruchin, Baldomero Navarro, Erica Maeda, Cláudia Inokuti

Structural and Civil Engineering Ernesto Tarnoczy Jr.

Mechanical and Electrical Engineering Eurico Freitas Marques

Interior Design FDE Team, Samuel Kruchin

Landscape Architecture Samuel Kruchin

Approximate Cost US$ 1,500,000

Site Area 3,542 m2

Building Area 3,200 m2

Total Floor Area 1,680 m2 - 1,771 m2

Brazil

Award Premiação IAB - Category: Edificações-Projeto

Given by Instituto de Arquitetos do Brasil

Prize presentation 1994

Architects **Sergio Pileggi / Euclides Oliveira, São Paulo**

Award Winning Building **Centro de Convençoes JCN**

Location São Paulo, Brazil

Brazil

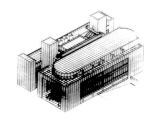

Award Premiação IAB/SP Building for Educacional Activities

Given by IAB/SP. Instituto de Arquitetos do Brasil

Prize Presentation March 1995

Members of the Jury Joaquim Guedes, Abrahão Sanovicz, Décio Tozzi, Gianfranco Vanucchi, Marília S. de Almeida, Tito Lívio Frascino

Architect **Rafael Antonio Cunha Perrone, São Paulo**

Award Winning Building **Creche Escola Jardim Estela / Daycare School**

Location Rua Pirambóia, Santo André, São Paulo, Brazil

Design and Construction Period 1991 -1992

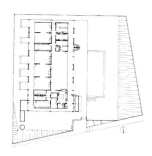

DesignTeam Rafael Antonio Cunha Perrone, Maria Cristina Junqueira, Maria Stella T. Bertaso, Mary Cristine Sakamoto

Structural and Civil Engineering Nicolau Cillurzo

Quantity Surveying City of Santo André Land Surveyors

Mechanical and Electrical Engineering Massayuki Taniguti

Landscape Architecture Rosana Chiarelli

Approximate Cost US$ 325,000

Site Area 2,900 m2

Building Area 810 m2

Total Floor Area 810 m2

Photography Hélio Corallo

Brazil

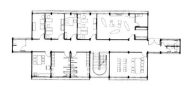

Award Premiação IAB/SP - Building for Healthcare Services
Given by IAB/SP. Instituto de Arquitetos do Brasil
Prize Presentation March 1995
Members of the Jury Architects: Joaquim Guedes, Abrahão Sanovicz, Décio Tozzi, Gianfranco Vanucchi, Marília S. de Almeida, Tito Lívio Frascino
Architect **Rafael Antonio Cunha Perrone, São Paulo**
Award Winning Building **Parque Miami - Posto de Saúde (Healthcare Services)**
Location Estrada do Pedroso, Santo André, São Paulo, Brazil
Design and Construction Period 1991 -1992

Design Team Rafael Antonio Cunha Perrone, Maria Cristina Junqueira, Maria Stella T. Bertaso, Mary Cristine Sakamoto
Structural and Civil Engineering Paulo Eduardo Fonseca Rodrigues, Nicolau Cillurzo
Quantity Surveying City of Santo André Land Surveyors
Mechanical and Electrical Engineering Otello Oliveri
Landscape Architecture City of Santo André Planning Gardens
Approximate Cost US$ 475,000
Site Area 3,960 m²
Building Area 650 m²
Total Floor Area 950 m²
Photography Hélio Corallo
Brazil

19

Award Premiação IAB - Category: Edificaçôes-Projeto
Given by Instituto de Arquitetos do Brasil
Prize Presentation 1994
Brazil

Architect **Adalberto Retto Júnior**
Award Winning Building **Edificio Residencial em Teffe**

Award Fremio ex-aequo IAB - Category: Arquitetura de Interiores-Ohra Executaca
Given by Instituto de Arquitetos do Brasil
Prize Presentation 1994
Brazil

Architect **Isay Weinfeld**
Award Winning Building **Loja Giovanna Baby**
Location Morumbi

C

Award Governor General's Award for Architecture
Architects **Dan S. Hanganu and Provencher Roy, Montréal**
Award Winning Building **Pointe-à-Callière, Musée d'Archéologie et d'Histoire de Montréal**
Canada

Page 82

Award Governor General's Award for Architecture
Architects **Richard Henriquez, Laszlo Nemeth Associates, Architects in Joint Venture, Vancouver**
Award Winning Building **Environmental Sciences Building, Trent University**
Canada

Page 86

Award Governor General's Award for Architecture
Architects **Kuwabara Payne McKenna Blumberg Architects, Toronto**
Award Winning Building **Reisman-Jenkinson House and Studio**
Canada

Page 90

Award Governor General's Award for Architecture
Given by The Governor General of Canada and the Royal Architectural
Institute of Canada
Prize Presentation October 1994
Members of the Jury Billie Tsien, Essy Baniassad, Raymond Moriyama,
Odile Hénault
Architect **Kuwabara Payne McKenna Blumberg, Toronto**
Award Winning Building **The Kitchener City Hall**
Location 200 King Street West, Kitchener, Ontario, Canada
Design and Construction Period winner of national competition
1989 - completed 1993

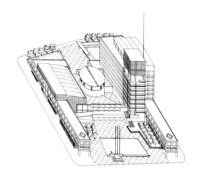

Design Team Bruce Kuwabara (Partner in charge), Marianne McKenna
(Partner), L. Larocca (Associate in charge), H. Sutcliffe
Structural and Civil Engineering Yolles Partnership Inc.
Quantity Surveying James F. Vermeulen Cost Consulting
Life Safety Consulting: Leber Rubes Inc.
Mechanical and Electrical Engineering mechanical: Merber Corporation,
electrical: Mulvey & Banani International Inc.
Interior Design Department Offices by Rice-Brydone Ltd.; all others
by KPMB Architects
Landscape Architecture Milus Bôllenberghe Topps Watchorn
Approximate Cost Can$ 43,000,000 for building
Building Area City Hall, offices and public Areas: 200,000 sq. ft.
Total Floor Area 400,000 sq. ft. for building (above and below grade)
Photography Steven Evans

Award Governor General's Award for Architecture
Given by The Royal Architectural Institute of Canada (RAIC)
and the Canada Council
Prize Presentation 1994
Members of the Jury Nigel Baldwin, Essy Baniassad, Odile Hénault,
Raymond Moriyama, Jeremy Sturgess, Billie Tsien
Architects **Oleson Worland Architects, Toronto**
Award Winning Building **The North Toronto Memorial Community Centre**
Location Eglinton Park, 200 Eglinton Ave. West, Toronto, Ontario, Canada
Design and Construction Period Summer 1986 - Spring 1993

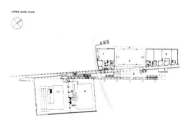

Design Team Core: R. Andrighetti, M. Michasiw (Project manager),
D. Oleson, W. Worland; R. Allen, Ch. Atkinson, M. Lavrisa,
R. Mar, Ch. Pearson, C. Racine, K. Rubinyi, A. Scott (Support)
Structural Engineering Yolles Partnership Ltd.
Quantity Surveying J. Vermeulen Cost Consultant Ltd.
Environmental Engineering Marshall Macklin Monaghan Ltd. (Skating
Rink Consultant)
Mechanical and Electrical Engineering Rybka Smith & Ginsler Ltd.
Landscape Architectureure Ferris + Quinn Associates Inc.
Approximate Cost Can$ 18,000,000
Site Area 23 acres
Building Area 30,000 sq. ft.
Total Floor Area 55,000 sq. ft. (excluding outdoor facilities and parking)
Photography Steven Evans

Award Governor General's Award for Architecture
Given by The Royal Architectural Institute of Canada
Canada

Prize Presentation 1994
Architect **John Patkau, Toronto**

Award Governor General's Award for Architecture
Given by The Royal Architectural Institute of Canada
Canada

Prize Presentation 1994
Architects **Brigitte Shim and Howard Sutcliffe, Toronto**

Award Mayor de la Ciudad
Given by La Federación Centroamericana de Arquitectos, Guatemala
Central America (Costa Rica, Guatemala, Honduras, Nicaragua, El Salvador)

Prize Presentation 1993
Architect **Roberto Ayinena Echeberria**

Award Premio Nacional de Arquitetura
Given by Colegio de Arquitectos de Chile
Chile

Prize Presentation September 1993
Architect **Christian de Groote**

Award Creation Awards of the Architectural Society of China between 1984-1993
Given by The Architectural Society of P.R.C.
Prize Presentation November 1993
Members of the Jury Members of the Architectural Society Council and the Appraise Committee
Architect **Liang Hongwen, School of Architecture, Shenzhen University**
Award Winning Building **The Performance and Conference Center of Shenzhen University**
Location Campus of Shenzhen University, Shenzhen, People's Republic of China
Design and Construction Period December 1987 - September 1988

Design Team Liang Hongwen with Lei Meigin, Huang Zhigang, Ou Zhiqirg, Wang Zhijie
Structural and Civil Engineering Chen Conglian and the Construction Group of Shenzhen University
Quantity Surveying The 6th Construction Company of Guangdong Province, P.R.C.
Environmental Engineering The Construction Group of Shenzhen University
Mechanical and Electrical Engineering Zhang Guangxian and the Construction Group of Shenzhen University
Interior Design Liang Hongwen
Landscape Architecture Liang Hongwen
Approximate Cost US$ 400,000
Site Area 6,000 m²
Building Area 4,000 m²
Total Floor Area 4,500 m²
Photography Liang Hongwen and Zhu lia Bas
People's Republic of China

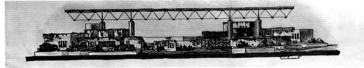

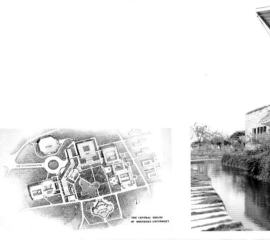

Award Creation Awards of the Architectural Society of China between the Years of 1988 - 1992
Architect **Zhang Jinqiu, Xian**
Award Winning Building **Shaanxi Historical Museum**
People's Republic of China

Page 94

Award National Excellent Design (Gold Award)
Given by Ministry of Construction
Prize Presentation 1993
Architect **Qi Kang, Head of Research Institute of Architecture, Southeast University, Nanjing**
Award Winning Building **Meiyuan Memorial Museum to the CPC Delegation**
Location Nanjing, People's Republic of China
Design and Construction Period 1991 - 1992

Design Team Qi Kang, Research Institute of Architecture, Southeast University, Nanjing
Structural and Civil Engineering Nanjing Institute of Architecture
Building Area 1,100 m^2 (ground floor)
People's Republic of China

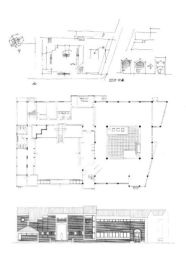

Award World Habitat Awards
Given by Building and Social Housing Foundation
Prize Presentation 1992
Architect **Liangyong Wu, Beijing**
Award Winning Building **Ju'er Hutong Housing**
Location Beijing, People's Republic of China
Design and Construction Period 1989 - 1993

Design Team Liangyong Wu and Institute for Architecture and Townplanning, Tsinghua University, Beijing
Structural and Civil Engineering Institute for Architecture and Design, Tsinghua University, Beijing
Landscape Architecture Liangyong Wu, Beijing
Building Area 12,550 m^2

People's Republic of China

Award Award of the ›Bienal Colombiana‹
Given by Sociedad Columbiana de Arquitectos
Columbia

Prize Presentation 1994
Architects **Fernando Rodriguez, Mario Daniel Mota**

Award Grand Prix of the Association of Czech Architects 1994
Architect **Roman Koucký, Prague**
Award Winning Building ***Re-cycling Centre with a Sewage Plant, Horní Maršov***

Czech Republic

Page 98

22

D

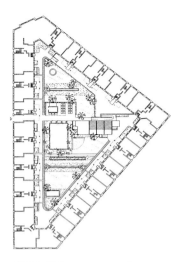

Award Den Grønne Nål

Given by DAL - The Federation of Danish Architects

Prize Presentation (time) 1995

Members of the Jury Charlotte Weile, Mogens Harttung, Rie Øhlenschlæger, Chris Svenningsen, Christian Poulsen

Architects **Tegnestuen DOMUS, Lyngby**

Award Winning Building **Urban Renewal in Kongens Enghave**

Location Borgbjergvej 1-13, Copenhagen SV, Denmark

Design and Construction Period 1993 -1994

Structural and Civil Engineering N & R Consult A/S

Environmental Engineering N & R Consult A/S

Mechanical and Electrical Engineering N & R Consult A/S

Landscape Architecture Tegnestuen DOMUS

Approximate Cost DKR 45,000,000

Site Area 4,500 m²

Building Area 2,400 m² (old and new)

Total Floor Area 12,000 m² (old and new)

Photography Svend Erik Andersen

Denmark

Award The Architectural Prize

Given by Danske Arkitekters Landsforbund

Prize Presentation 1995

Architect **Elsebeth Gerner Nielsen**

Denmark

Award Den Grønne Nål

Given by The Federation of Danish Architects DAL

Prize Presentation May 1995

Members of the Jury Michael Sten Johnson, Annette Brunsvig Soerensen, Chris Fløe Svenningsen, Lone Wiggers, Soeren Boegh, Henny Green, Johan Fogh, all architects of DAL

Architects **Gruppen for by- og landskabsplanlægning aps - architects, planners and Landscape Architectures, Kolding**

Award Winning Building **Architect's Office, Kolding; here: Urban Renewal**

Location Kolding, Denmark

Design and Construction Period 1992 -1994

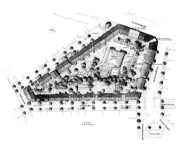

Design Team Gruppen for by - og landskabsplanlægning aps; Torben Gade, Inge Bauer, Lillian Toftdal

Structural and Civil Engineering A/S Samfundsteknik

Landscape Architecture Gruppen for by - og landskabsplanlægning aps

Approximate Cost DKR 13,000,000 (approx. ECU 1,625,000)

Site Area 5000 m²

Building Area 425 m²

Total Floor Area 700 m²

Photography Torben Gade

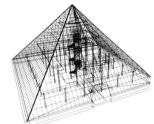

Denmark

E

Award IX Bienal Panamericana de Arquitectura de Quito - Categoria de
Conservacion, Preservacion, Restauracion y Adaptacion a Nuevo Uso del
Patrimonio Edificado
Given by Colegio de Arquitectos del Ecuador
Prize Presentation November 1994
Members of the Jury Juan B. Artigas, Juvenile Barrack, Francisco Naranjo
Architects **Marcela Alemán (Ecuador) and Patrick de Sutter (Belgium)**
Award Winning Building **Convent Maxim de Santo Domingo**
Location Historical Center of Quito, Ecuador
Design and Construction Period 1991 -1994

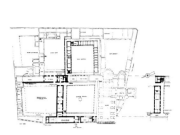

Design Team Project Ecuador-Belgium: M. Alemán, Patrick de Sutter,
L. Galeas, F. Acosta, J. Loor
Structural and Civil Engineering K. van Balen, M. León, Gavilanes,
J. C. Izurieta
Quantity Surveying Raymond Lemaire, K. van Balen
Mechanical and Electrical Engineering L. Pesantez, R. Barragán
Interior Design L. Galeas, F. Acosta, F. Olmedo
Landscape Architecture Taller Quito 1
Approximate Cost BFr 2,700,000 for Belgium; 350,000,000 Sucres
for Ecuador
Site Area 22,100 m²
Building Area 15,738 m²
Total Floor Area 32,447 m²
Total Area for intervention 2,700 m²

Ecuador

Award IX Bienal Panamericana de Arquitectura de Quito - Categoria de
Conservacion, Preservacion, Restauracion y Adaptacion a Nuevo Uso del
Patrimonio Edificado, Mencion de Honor Nacional
Given by Colegio de Arquitectos del Ecuador

Prize Presentation November 1994
Architects **Carvajal / Fondello**
Award Winning Building **Casa de los Siete Patios, Quito,**
Rehabilitacion de Vivienda

Ecuador

Award IX Bienal Panamericana de Arquitectura de Quito, Mencion De Honor
Given by Colegio de Arquitectos del Ecuador
Prize Presentation November 1994
Members of the Jury J. Guedes, Espinosa
Architects **Hariri & Hariri Architects, New York**
Award Winning Building **The New Canaan House**
Location New Canaan, Connecticut, USA
Design and Construction Period 1990 -1993

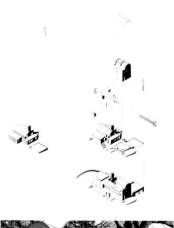

Design Team Gisue Hariri, Mojgan Hariri; Partners in charge: Andre Bideau,
Yves Habegger, Kazem Naderi, Willliam Wilson
Structural Engineering Ahneman Associates
Mechanical and Electrical Engineering GOL Construction
Interior Design Donna Gorman
Approximate Cost US$ 150 per sq. ft.
Site Area 2 acres
Building Area 3,800 sq. ft.
Total Floor Area 3,100 sq. ft.
Photography John Hall

Ecuador

Award Architectural Design Grand Award

Architects **Mitchell / Giurgola Architects, in association with Rancorn Wildman, Krause and Brezinski**

Award Winning Building **Virginia Air and Space Center**

Page 100

Ecuador _____

Award IX Bienal Panamericana de Arquitectura de Quito, Mencion De Honor

Given by Colegio de Arquitectos del Ecuador

Prize Presentation November 1994

Members of the Jury J. Guedes, F. Espinosa, E. Yanes, H. de Garay, A. Saldarriaga

Architects **Alfredo Ribadeneira, Henry Carrion, Quito**

Award Winning Building **Apartamentos Andino**

Location Quito, Ecuador

Design and Construction Period 1993 -1994

Structural and Civil Engineering Francisco Nuñez

Interior Design Una Idea

Landscape Architectureure Plantnar

Approximate Cost US$ 490,000

Site Area 1,200 m²

Building Area 1,656 m²

Total Floor Area 670 m²

Ecuador _____

Award Gran Premio Internacional IX Bienal Panamericana de Arquitectura de Quito

Architect **Jorge Rigamonti, Caracas, Venezuela**

Award Winning Building **Campamento Turístico Cayo Crasquí**

Page 104

Ecuador _____

Award II. Prize and Medal at the International Contest ›Best Architectural Work of 1993‹

Given by International Association of Architects, Unions of the CIS Countries, IAAU

Prize Presentation November 1993

Members of the Jury R. Karimov (Chairman), B. Nelubin, E. Kovalevski, F. Ashrafi, A. Bekjancf, A. Badalian, D. Omualiev, T. Abramova

Architects **Sarkis Sardarian and Rusanna Mamian, Erevan**

Award Winning Building **Villages Arpeni and Goghovit in the Earthquake Zone**

Location Ashotsk Region, Armenia

Design and Construction Period 1989 - 1991

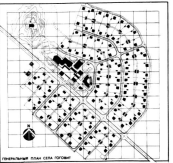

Structural and Civil Engineering V. O. Hovasapian, L. Tumanian, K. Ohanjanian

Quantity Surveying Firm ›Nakhagits‹

Environmental Engineering A. Petrosian, E. Kocharian

Mechanical and Electrical Engineering Z. Mirjeferjian, L. Agajanian

Interior Design S. Sardarian, R. Mamian

Landscape Architectureure V. Bagramian, H. Martirosian

Approximate Cost Arpeni: US$ 10,300,000; Goghovit: US$ 9,400,000

Site Area Arpeni: 25 ha, Goghovit: 21 ha

Building Area Arpeni: 12,650 m², Goghovit: 10,350 m² (dwelling)

Arpeni: 3,850 m², Goghovit: 3,520 m² (civic building)

Photography Sarkis Sardarian, Rusanna Mamian

Eurasian Group (Armenia) _____

Award Grand Prix of Architecture, Construction and Design
Given by IAAU
Eurasian Group (Armenia)

Prize Presentation November / 2 /1993
Architects **A.N. Kolontai, A.G. Turusov, A.J. Tschadowitch**

Award Grand Prix of Architecture, Construction and Design
Given by IAAU
Eurasian Group (Armenia)

Prize Presentation November / 2 /1993
Architects **M.Ch. Vachidow, A.L. Onischtschenko, D.W. Latipov**

F

Award Alvar Aalto Medal
Given by Finnish Association of Architects
Prize Presentation October / 24 /1992
Finland

Architect **Glenn Murcutt**
Awarded for his Life Work

Award Equerre d'Argent - Mention
Given by Le Moniteur
Prize Presentation 1994
Members of the Jury Mario Botta, Jean Nouvel, Michael Hopkins, Maarten
Kloos, Jacques Lucan, Marc N. Vigier, Nicola di Battista
Architect **Philippe Gazeau, Paris**
Award Winning Building **Logements pour postiers**
Location 26 Rue de l'Ourcq, Paris
Design and Construction Period 1992 -1994

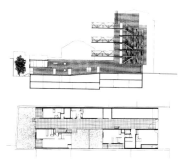

Structural and Civil Engineering M. Mimram
Mechanical and Electrical Engineering C FERM
Approximate Cost FF 18,000,000
Site Area 700 m²
Building Area 1,260 m²
Total Floor Area 2,300 m²
Photography Jean-Marie Monthiers
France

Award Mention au Prix de la Première Oeuvre
Given by Le Moniteur
Prize Presentation October 1994
Members of the Jury Marc N. Vigier, Michael Hopkins, Mario Botta, Jean
Nouvel, Nicola di Battista, Maarten Kloos, Jaques Lucan, René Eladari
Architect **Xavier Leibar, Ciboure**
Award Winning Building **Ikastola, Basque School**
Location Biarritz, France
Design and Construction Period April 1992 - October 1993

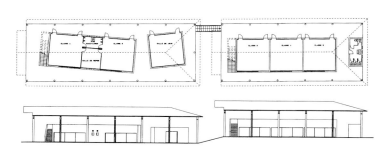

Design Team Xavier Leibar, Jean-Marie Seigneurin
Structural and Civil Engineering Cobet, ECTA
Quantity Surveying Jean Bariac, CEP
Environmental Engineering CBI
Approximate Cost FF 3,250,000 (tax free)
Building Area 525 m²
Total Floor Area 1,500 m²
Photography Xavier Leibar, Dominique Delaunay
France

26

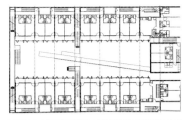

Award Equerre d'Argent
Given by Le Moniteur
Prize Presentation 1994
Architects **François Marzelle, Isabelle Manescau, Edouard Steeg**
Award Winning Building **Résidence Foyer**
Location Rue Poyenne, Bordeaux
Design and Construction Period design: May - October 1991; planning permission: June 1992; construction: July 1993 - August 1994

Electrical Engineering Enelat
Approximate Cost FF 16,900,000
Building Area 2,520 m² (logements)
Photography Vincent Monthiers

France ———

Award 1- Second Prize for Town-Planning 1990 / 2- Special Prize of the ›Equerre d'Argent‹ 1995
Given by 1- Fondation of the Academy of Architecture; 2- The Journal Moniteur
Architect **Dominique Perrault, Paris**
Award Winning Building **Bibliothèque nationale de Paris**

Page 106

France ———

Award Grand Prix National d'Architecture
Given by Ministry of Infrastructures, Transport and Tourism
Prize Presentation November /16 /1993
Members of the Jury Jean Frébault (President), Jean Bousquet, Roland Schweitzer, Christian de Portzamparc, Christian Hauvette, Élisabeth Allain-Dupré, Richard Rogers, Aurelio Galfetti, Manuel Gausa

Architect **Dominique Perrault, Paris**
Award Winning Building **in recognition of the entire work of Dominique Perrault**

France ———

Award Yearly ›Moniteur de l'Architecture‹ Award 1992; selected for the National Prize List of the twelve more representative projects of the Year 1993
Architect **Eric Raffy, Bordeaux**
Award Winning Building **Michel Bras Hotel and Restaurant**

Location Laguiole, France
Design and Construction Period 1992
Approximate Cost US$ 4,000,000

France ———

G

Award Der große BDA-Preis (Gold Medal)
Architect **Thomas Herzog, Munich**
Award Winning Building **in recognition of the entire work of Thomas Herzog; here: Design Center Linz**

Page 112

Germany ———

H

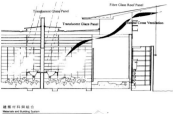

Award Annual Award 1994 (President's Prize)

Given by The Hong Kong Institute of Architects, HKIA

Prize Presentation March 1995

Members of the Jury Kenneth Kan Cho Yau, Dominic Kwan Wing Hong, Tunney Lee Chan Fai, Helena To Hiu Ming, Victor So Wing Tong, Helen Yu Lai Ching Ping

Architects **Lo Kin Leung, Wallace Chang Ping Hung, Lo Chi Sing, Hong Kong**

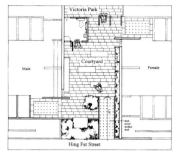

Award Winning Building **Public Toilet at Hing Fat Street**

Location Causeway Bay, Hong Kong

Design and Construction Period October 1992 - February 1994

Design Team Lo Kin Leung, Wallace Chang Ping Hung, Lo Chi Sing

Structural and Civil Engineering Ove Arup & Partners

Quantity Surveying Levett & Bailey Chartered

Mechanical and Electrical Engineering Meinhardt (M&E) Ltd.

Approximate Cost HK$ 4,171,273.25

Site Area 120 m²

Building Area 120 m²

Total Floor Area 120 m²

Photography Keith Chan

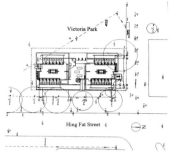

Award ARCASIA Gold Medal Award

Given by The Architects Regional Council Asia

Prize Presentation December 1994

Members of the Jury R. Alcordo, R. Punzalan, A. Ng

Architects **Rocco Design Partners, Hong Kong**

Award Winning Building **Lok Fu Shopping Centre II**

Location Lok Fu, Junction Road, Kowloon, Hong Kong

Design and Construction Period 1987 -1991

Design Team Rocco Yim, Bernard Hui, Patrick Lee, Calvin Ho, Timothy Yuen

Structural and Civil Engineering Harris & Sutherland (F. E.) Ltd.

Quantity Surveying Levett & Bailey

Mechanical and Electrical Engineering Associated Consulting Engineering

Interior Design Rocco Design Partners

Landscape Architecture Housing Department

Approximate Cost HK$ 200,000,000 (US$ 25,000,000)

Site Area 12,00 m²

Building Area 3,500 m²

Total Floor Area 15,000 m²

Photography Rocco Design Partners

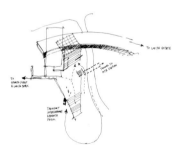

Award HKIA Silver Medal

Given by The Hong Kong Institute of Architects

Prize Presentation March 1995

Members of the Jury T. Lee, Helen Yu, Victor So, Helena To, Kenneth Kan

Architects **Rocco Design Partners, Hong Kong**

Award Winning Building **Citibank Plaza**

Location 3 Garden Road, Central, Hong Kong

Design and Construction Period 1989 - 1992

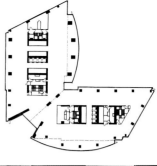

Design Team Rocco Yim, Patrick Lee, Bernard Hui,
C. M. Chan, Hector Cheung, David Wong, Trilby Choi

Structural and Civil Engineering Ove Arups & Partners

Quantity Surveying Levett & Bailey

Mechanical and Electrical Engineering J. Roger Preston & Partners

Interior Design Rocco Design Partners

Landscape Architecture Urbis Travers Morgan Ltd.

Approximate Cost US$ 225,000,000

Site Area 8,600 m²

Building Area 4,500 m²

Total Floor Area 154,000 m²

Photography Rocco Design Partners

Award Certificate of Merit 1994

Architects **Wong Tung & Partners Limited, Hong Kong**

Award Winning Building **Dragon Centre**

Page 116

Hong Kong

Award Ybl Miklós Prize

Given by Ministry for Environment and Regional Policy

Prize Presentation July / 1 / 1994

Architect **Zoltán Csikós, Budapest**

Award Winning Building **all projects; here: Kitchens of the Institute for Psychiatry and Neurology**

Design and Construction Period 1990 - 1993

Building Area 4,857 m²

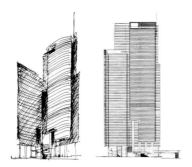

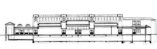

Hungary

Award Pro Architectura Prize
Given by Ministry for Environment and Regional Policy
Prize Presentation July / 1 / 1994
Members of the Jury Szabolcs Pataky, Imre Kovács, Imre Körmendy, Zsolt Jékely, János Mónus, Lajos Zalaváry, József Kerényi, Tibor Mikolás
Architect **Tamás Czigány, Györ**
Award Winning Building **›Apor Vilmos‹ Catholic School Centre**
Location Györ, Hungary
Design and Construction Period 1990 - 1993

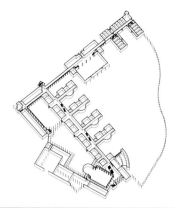

Design Team DIMENZIÓ Consulting, Tamás Czigány, József Fodróczy, István F. Varga
Structural and Civil Engineering DIMENZIÓ Consulting, Péter Szabó, Daysi Mester
Quantity Surveying Jenö Gábor
Environmental Engineering Vince Pongrácz, Erzsébet Pintér
Mechanical and Electrical Engineering Zoltán Gyurkovics, József Décsi
Interior Design Csaba Z. Szabó
Landscape Architecture Magdolna Csemez
Approximate Cost HUF 500,000,000
Site Area 35,000 m²
Building Area 9,300 m²
Total Floor Area 12,200 m²
Photography István Ö. Mezödy, Tamás Czigány

Hungary

Award Pro Architectura Prize
Given by The Chamber and Association of Hungarian Architects
Hungary

Prize Presentation 1995
Architect **Sándor Dévényi, Pécs**

Award Ybl Miklós Prize
Architect **Dezső Ekler**
Award Winning Building **All projects; here: Cultural Camp in Nagykálló**
Hungary

Page 120

Award Pro Architectura Prize
Given by The Chamber and Association of Hungarian Architects
Hungary

Prize Presentation 1995
Architect **Gábor Farkas, Keoekemét**

Award Ybl Miklós Prize
Given by The Chamber and Association of Hungarian Architects
Hungary

Prize Presentation 1995
Architect **Gabor Locsmandi, Budapest**

Award Pro Architectura Prize
Given by The Chamber and Association of Hungarian Architects
Hungary

Prize Presentation 1995
Architect **Otto Luchesi, Soeymár**

I

Award IAI Award for Architects and their Buildings
Given by Indonesian Institute of Architects
Indonesia

Prize Presentation 1993
Architect **Y. B. Mangunwijaya, Yogyakarta (Central-Java)**

Award IAI Award for Individuals (Architects & Non-Architects) & Institutions
Given by Indonesian Institute of Architects

Indonesia _____

Prize Presentation September 1993
Architects **Triadi Cokro & Tini Senjaya, Jakarta**

Award RIAI Regional Award (Dublin)
Given by The Royal Institute of the Architects of Ireland
Prize Presentation 1994

Ireland _____

Architects **Burke-Kennedy Doyle & Partners, Dublin**
Award Winning Building **St. Francis Hospice, Station Road**
Location Dublin, Ireland

Award RIAI Regional Award (Southern)
Given by The Royal Institute of the Architects of Ireland
Prize Presentation 1994

Ireland _____

Architect **De Paor O'Neill, Dublin**
Award Winning Building **Visitor Building, Royal Gunpowder Mills**
Location Ballincollig, Ireland

Award RIAI Regional Award (Northern)
Given by The Royal Institute of the Architects of Ireland
Prize Presentation 1994
Architects **Kennedy FitzGerald and Associates, Belfast**

Ireland _____

Award Winning Building **The Aquatic Science Research Division Building**
Location Belfast, Ireland
Design and Construction Period 1993 - 1994

Award RIAI Regional Awards (Northern)
Given by The Royal Institute of the Architects of Ireland
Prize Presentation June / 14 / 1994
Architects **Kennedy FitzGerald and Associates, Belfast**
Award Winning Building **Dungannon Leisure Centre, for Dungannon District Council**
Location Dungannon, North Ireland
Design and Construction Period 3 years

Design Team J. Kennedy, N. Hatchinson, J. Keane
Structural and Civil Engineering Kirk McClure Morton
Quantity Surveying Hood Magowan Kirk
Environmental Engineering The Caldwell Partnership
Mechanical and Electrical Engineering The Caldwell Partnership
Landscape Architecture Dungannon District Council
Approximate Cost £ 2,000,000
Site Area 1.5 ha
Building Area 1,800 m²
Total Floor Area 3,000 m²

Ireland _____

Award RIAI Regional Award (Northern)
Given by The Royal Institute of the Architects of Ireland
Prize Presentation 1994

Ireland _____

Architects **McAdam Design, Belfast**
Award Winning Building **Navan Visitor Centre, 81 Killylea Road**
Location Armagh, Ireland

Award RIAI Regional Award (Eastern)

Given by The Royal Institute of the Architects of Ireland

Prize Presentation April 1994

Members of the Jury John Hejduk - Dean of Cooper Union, New York

Architects **National Building Agency Ltd., Dublin**

Award Winning Building **Residential Quarter at St. Peter's Port, Athlone**

Location Athlone, Co Westmeath, Ireland

Design and Construction Period 1991 -1993

Design Team M. V. Cullinan NBA

Structural and Civil Engineering Ed. Hanlon, Peter Fay

Quantity Surveying John McKinney

Approximate Cost IR £ 550,000

Site Area 43 acres

Building Area townhouse: 87 m², apartment: 65 m²

Total Floor Area 950 m²

Ireland _____

Award 1- Award for Architectural Excellence / 2- RIAI Regional Award
(Western)

Architects **The Office of Public Works Architects, Dublin**

Award Winning Building **The Céide Fields Visitor Centre**

Page 124

Ireland _____

Award RIAI Regional Award (Southern)

Architects **The Office of Public Works Architects, Dublin**

Award Winning Building **The Blasket Island Cultural Centre**

Page 126

Ireland _____

Award RIAI Regional Award (Dublin)

Given by The Royal Institute of the Architects of Ireland

Prize Presentation June 1994

Members of the Jury Deirdre O'Connor (Chairperson), Tom Carr,
Joe Fitzgerald, Neil Hegarty, Ken Meehan, Duncan O'Kelly

Architects **Murray O'Laoire Associates, Limerick**

Award Winning Building **Extension to Leo Laboratories**

Location 285 Cashel Rd., Crumlin, Dublin 12, Ireland

Design and Construction Period June 1991 - March 1993

Design Team Murray O'Laoire Associates: Sean O'Laoire (Partner-in-charge), Calbhac O'Carroll (Design architect), Patrick Cassidy (Project architect),
Mark O'Mahony, Tom Creed, Hugh Kelly (Assistants)

Structural and Civil Engineering Horgan Lynch + Partners,
Partner-in-charge: Frank Murray, assistant: Michael Shorthall

Quantity Surveying Healy Kelly & Partners

Environmental Engineering EMA Ltd.

Mechanical and Electrical Engineering DPS Engineering

Interior Design Murray O'Laoire Associates

Landscape Architecture Gerry Mitchell & Associates

Approximate Cost IR £ 3,500,000

Building Area 18,000 sq. ft.

Total Floor Area 1,582 m²

Photography Arc Survey Photography Ltd.

Ireland _____

Award RIAI Regional Award (Southern)
Given by The Royal Institute of the Architects of Ireland
Prize Presentation 1994
Ireland

Architects **Reg Chandler & Partners, Dublin**
Award Winning Building **Ballybunion Golf Club**
Location Ballybunion, Ireland

Award RIAI Regional Award (Dublin)
Given by The Royal Institute of the Architects of Ireland
Prize Presentation 1994
Ireland

Architect **Scott Tallon Walker, Dublin**
Award Winning Building **Biotechnology Centre, University College**
Location Dublin, Ireland

Award Zeev Rechter Prize
Given by Israel Society of Architects and Town Planners
Prize Presentation 1994
Architect **Shlomo Aronson**
Israel

Award Winning Building **The Place of the Neve Zedek Dance and Theater Center in Tel Aviv**
Location Tel Aviv, Israel

Award Zeev Rechter Prize
Given by Israel Society of Architects and Town Planners
Prize Presentation 1993
Members of the Jury Shlomo Aronson, Zeev Drokman, Moshe Zur
Architect **Moshe Atsmon, Tel Aviv**
Award Winning Building **Tel Aviv University Entrance Complex**
Location Tel Aviv, Israel
Design and Construction Period 4 years

33

Design Team Moshe Atsmon (Head of team), Y. Eldan
Structural and Civil Engineering Horovitz-Buch-Engineering
Quantity Surveying A. Y. Halperin
Mechanical and Electrical Engineering Y. Shtarzer
Interior Design E. Yeshay
Landscape Architecture M. Atsmon, Moriya-Sekely
Approximate Cost US$ 9,000,000
Site Area 13,000 m²
Building Area 2,000 m²
Total Floor Area 5,000 m²
Photography Ran Erde
Israel

Award Zeev Rechter Prize
Given by Israel Society of Architects and Town Planners
Israel

Prize Presentation December 1994
Architects **Ulrich Pelsner and Dan Veinman, Jerusalem**

Award Architecture Prize on 1st of July
Given by Israel Society of Architects and Town Planners
Israel

Prize Presentation December 1994
Architects **Arthur Spector and Micha Amisar, Jerusalem**

J

Award JIA Award for the Best Young Architect of the Year
Given by The Japan Institute of Architects (JIA)
Prize Presentation 1993
Architects **Taro Ashihara Architects, Tokyo**
Award Winning Building **Kasama Nichido Museum of Art**
Location Kasama City, Japan
Japan

Design and Construction Period 1988 - 1989

Design Team Taro Ashihara, Mamoru Yahata, Kunihiro Ueda
Structural and Civil Engineering Sadao Ariyama
Mechanical and Electrical Engineering Inuzuka Engineering Consultants
Site Area 925,39 m²

Award JIA Award for the Best Young Architect of the Year
Architect **Hiroshi Miyazaki, Tokyo**

Japan

Award Annual Architectural Design Commendation of the Japan Institute
of Architects
Given by The Japan Institute of Architects (JIA)
Prize Presentation May / 30 / 1995
Members of the Jury Mitsuru Senda, Osamu Ishiyama, Kunihide Onomi,
Nobuo Hozumi

Architect **Shuntaro Noda, Tokyo**

Award Winning Building **Dormitory for the Yoshikawa Oil-Recycle
Company**

Location Hikoma, Tanuma-Machi, Aso-Gun, Tochigi, Japan
Design and Construction Period Design: August 1989 - November 1991;
Construction: May 1992 - October 1993

Design Team Jin Architects & Associates
Structural and Civil Engineering Arai Structural Design Studio
Mechanical and Electrical Engineering Lina M & E Planning
Landscape Architecture Bunji Kaneko
Approximate Cost 300,000,000 Yen (US$ 3,000,000)
Site Area 5,501.70 m²
Building Area 1,685 m²
Total Floor Area 1,637.17 m²

Award Winning Building **Chuya Nakahara Memorial Museum**
Page 128

Award JIA Award for the Best Young Architect of the Year
Architect **Tadasu Ohe, Tokyo**

Japan

Award JIA Award for the Best Young Architect of the Year
Given by The Japan Institute of Architects (JIA)
Prize Presentation 1993
Members of the Jury Seizoh Sakata, Kohichi Sone, Akira Kuryu

Architect **Hidetoshi Ohno, Tokyo**

Award Winning Building **Headquarters & Auditorium for NBK
Seki Garden Factory**

Location Kurachi Mukohyama, Seki-shi, Gihu
Design and Construction Period Design: August 1989 - February 1991;
Construction: March 1991 - May 1992

Design Team Hidetoshi Ohno + Architects & Planners League
Structural and Civil Engineering Hanawa Structural Engineering
Quantity Surveying Takanawa Kenchiku Jimusho Co.Ltd
Mechanical and Electrical Engineering Sogo Consultants
Acoustic Engineering Nagata Acoustics Inc.
Interior Design Hidetoshi Ohno
Landscape Architecture Hidetoshi Ohno
Approximate Cost 900,000,000 Yen
Site Area 71,876 m²
Building Area 1,475 m²
Total Floor Area 2,023 m²
Photography Toshiyuki Kitajima

Japan

Award Winning Building **Fun House**
Page 134

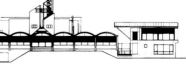

Award Special Award for Design Excellence
Given by Asia Pacific Interior Design Awards
Prize Presentation 1994
Architect **Eric Raffy, Bordeaux**
Award Winning Building **Jodo Buddha**
Location Ushiku-Arcadia site
Interior Design Eric Raffy
Approximate Cost US$ 4,000,000

Japan

K

Award Le Prix de l'Union des Architectes de la République du Kazakhstan
Given by Union des Architectes de la République du Kazakhstan
Kazakhstan

Prize Presentation 1993
Architect **Säoumenov Akjäik, Almaty**

Award Le Prix de l'Union des Architèctes de la République du Kazakhstan
Architect **Alberto Campo Baeza, Madrid**
Kazakhstan

Award Winning Building **Looking at the sea, Public School**
Page 138

35

Award Shilling Award
Given by The Architectural Association of Kenya
Prize Presentation May 1992
Members of the Jury R.G.M. Mutiso (Chairman), James G. Waweru,
David Njuguna, Geoffrey N. Githunguri, Kimani Mathu, Austin Kitololo,
James Gitoho and Kuria Gathoni
Architect **Dalgliesh Marshall Johnson, Nairobi**
Award Winning Building **International Laboratory for Research on
Animal Diseases (now amalgamated with ILRI)**
Location Kabete, Kenia
Design and Construction Period 1976 - 1978 (original campus), 1987 - 1995
(subsequent works)

Design Team R. Marshall, P. Hepple, M. Neill & S. Johnson
Structural and Civil Engineering Ishwar Patel, H. S. Sura
Quantity Surveying Mike Charles, Bashir Hajee
Environmental Engineering Richard Kristiansen, M. Thomsen, H. S. Sura
Interior Design Per Geheb
Landscape Architecture Melanie Richards
Approximate Cost $ 7,500,000 (original campus) $ 4,000,000
(subsequent works)
Site Area 69 ha
Building Area 15,400 m² (original campus), 3,247 m² (subsequent works)
Total Floor Area 18,647 m²
Photography Derek Pegrume

Kenya

Award Shilling Award
Given by The Architectural Association of Kenya
Kenya

Prize Presentation 1994
Architect **Mutiso Menezes International, Nairobi**

Japan · Kazakhstan · Kenya

Award Shilling Award

Given by Architectural Association of Kenya

Kenya

Prize Presentation 1994

Architects **Planning Systems Services, Nairobi**

L

Award Prix Luxembourgeois d'Architecture

Architects **Hermann & Valentiny, Architectes, Vienna / Luxembourg**

Luxembourg / Austria

Award Winning Building **Luxembourg Embassy, Vienna**

Page 142

M

Award / Recommendation of Chamber of Architects and Civil Engineers

Architect **Architecture Project**

Malta

Award Winning Building **Corporate Offices for L. Farrugio and Sons Ltd.**

Page 146

Award Award of the Ministère de l'Habitat / ERAC Oriental

Given by Ministère de l'Habitat / ERAC Oriental

Prize Presentation March 1994

Architect **Jaouad Msefar, Casablanca**

Award Winning Building **Ville Nouvelle de Selouane**

Location Selouane, Morocco

Morocco

N

Award Award of Merit: Engraved Plaque & Certificate of Merit

Given by Namibia Institute of Architects

Prize Presentation August 1995

Members of the Jury K. Afshani, K. Brandt, J. Wasserfall, T. Tuomari

Architects **Kerry McNamara Architects Inc., Windhoek**

Award Winning Building **First National Bank of Namibia, Head Office &**

Windhoek Branch (refurbishment and renovation)

Location Windhoek, Namibia

Design and Construction Period 36 months

Design Team Kerry McNamara Architects Inc.

Structural and Civil Engineering Arup Namibia

Quantity Surveying Wicks, Goosen & Pineo

Mechanical and Electrical Engineering mechanical: Bicon Namibia;

electrical: Juliohn Taylor Consulting Engineering

Approximate Cost US$ 4,000,000

Site Area 1,653 m²

Building Area 1,320 m²

Total Floor Area 3,420 m²

Photography D. Fourie

Republic of Namibia

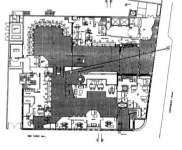

36

Award Grand Prix Rhénan d'Architecture
Given by A.D.C.A. Strasbourg / France
Prize Presentation June 1993
Members of the Jury Henri Ciriani, Paolo Fumagati, Andy Raeber,
H. Jan Tennekes, At Tuns, Helmut Striffler, Günther Frantz
Architect **Herman Hertzberger, Amsterdam**
Award Winning Building **Extension Primary School for the School
Association ›Aerdenhout Bentveld‹**
Location Aerdenhout, The Netherlands
Design and Construction Period 1988 -1989

Structural and Civil Engineering Ingenieursbureau Damen, The Hague
Interior Design Architectuurstudio Herman Hertzberger
Landscape Architecture Architectuurstudio Herman Hertzberger
Approximate Cost Hfl 1,250,000
Site Area approx. 3,350 m²
Building Area approx. 765 m² (old: 330 m²; new: 435 m²)
Total Floor Area approx. 1,193 m² (old: 438 m²; new: 755 m²)
Photography Herman Hertzberger, Colette Sloots, Ger van der Vlugt

The Netherlands _____

Award Anton Christian Houens Fonds Diplom
Given by Culture Department of Norway
Prize Presentation October 1994
Members of the Jury Norske Arkitekters Landsforbund's Comitee for
A. C. Houens Fonds Diplom
Architects **KS Per Knudsen Arkitektkontor AS, Trondheim**
Award Winning Building **Medisinsk Teknisk Senter**
Location Trondheim, Norway
Design and Construction Period 1988 - 1991

 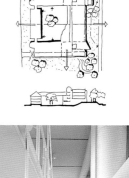

Design Team Øysten Hoffart, Per Knudsen, Jan Støring
Structural and Civil Engineering Karl Knudsen AS
Quantity Surveying KS Per Knudsen Arkitektkontor AS and Technical
Engineering
Environmental Engineering Gaute Flatheim AS
Mechanical and Electrical Engineering IGP AS
Interior Design KS Per Knudsen Arkitektkontor AS
Landscape Architecture KS Per Knudsen Arkitektkontor AS
Approximate Cost NOK 89,700,000 (building), NOK 146,000,000 (total)
Site Area 9,450 m²
Building Area 3,130 m²
Total Floor Area 15,285 m² (new building), 1,500 m² (old building)
Photography Øhlander

Norway

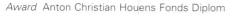

Award Anton Christian Houens Fonds Diplom
Given by Norske Arkitekters Landsforbund
Prize Presentation October 1994
Members of the Jury Norske Arkitekters Landsforbund's Comittee for
A. C. Houens Fonds Diplom
Architects **Lund & Slaatto Arkitekter AS by Kjell Lund, Oslo**
Award Winning Building **Sølvberget Culture House**
Location Stavanger, Norway
Design and Construction Period 1980 - 1987

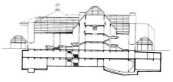

Structural and Civil Engineering Kristoffer Apeland
Environmental Engineering Flatheim AS
Mechanical and Electrical Engineering Aarskog, Mjelde og Johannesen AS
Landscape Architecture Stavanger Local Council
Approximate Cost NOK 220,000,000
Site Area approx. 3,000 m²
Building Area approx. 3,000 m²
Total Floor Area 15,370 m²
Photography Jon Haug, Lund & Slaatto Arkitekter AS

Norway

Award European Steel Design Award
Given by European Convention of Constructional Steelwork
Prize Presentation Cologne, September / 13 / 1995
Architects **Lund & Slaatto Arkitekter AS, Oslo**
Award Winning Building **Nordhordlandsbrua**
Location Salhusfjord, Bergen, Norway
Design and Construction Period March 1990 - September 1994

Design Team Kjell Lund & Nils Slaatto / Lunde & Løvseth
Structural and Civil Engineering The Municipal Highways Office and
Aas-Jacobsen, Veritec
Landscape Architecture Hindhamar, Sundt and Thomassen
Approximate Cost NOK 910,000,000

Norway

P

Award Best Midsize Apartment Building of the Year 1994
Given by Sociedad Panameña de Ingenieros y Arquitectos
Prize Presentation October 1995
Members of the Jury Alberto W. Osorio, José Batista, Valentín Monforte
Architects **Edwin Brown Castro, Punta Paitilla**
Award Winning Building **Royal Princess Condominium**
Location Urbanización Punta Paitilla, Panama City, Panama
Design and Construction Period August 1992 - November 1994

Design Team Edwin Brown & Asociados
Structural and Civil Engineering Alberto Bermúdez & Adolfo Quelquejeu
Mechanical and Electrical Engineering Carlos Penna
Approximate Cost US$ 5,500,000
Site Area 1,200 m²
Building Area 9,333.70 m² (apartments), 4,415.70 m² (exteriors and
parking)
Total Floor Area 13,749.40 m²
Photography Edwin Brown

Panama

Award Best Large Apartment Building of the Year 1994
Given by Sociedad Panameña de Ingenieros y Arquitectos
Prize Presentation October 1995
Members of the Jury Alberto W. Osorio, José Batista, Valentín Monforte
Architects **Edwin Brown Castro, Punta Paitilla**
Award Winning Building **Bayside Tower Condominium**
Location Winston Churchill St., Punta Paitilla, Panama City, Panama
Design and Construction Period April 1992 - May 1994

Design Team Edwin Brown C., Linet Vanesa de Brown
Structural and Civil Engineering Victor Cano
Mechanical and Electrical Engineering O. Vallarino & R. De La Guardia
Approximate Cost US$ 6,400,000
Site Area 1,240 m²
Building Area 14,744 m² (apartments), 5,858 m² (exteriors and parking)
Total Floor Area 20,602 m²

Panama

Award Hexagono de Oro, VIII Bienal de Arquitectura
Architects **Oscar Borasino, Jose Antonio Vallarino, Miraflores**
Award Winning Building **Chapel of the Reconciliation**

Page 166

Peru

39

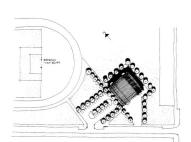

Award 1- Hexagono de Plata a Mejor Estructura / 2- Hexagono de Plata
a Mejor Uso Materiales

Given by Colegio de Arquitectos del Perú

Prize Presentation 1992 - 1993

Members of the Jury Colegio de Arquitectos

Architect **Jorge Burga Bartra, Lima**

Award Winning Building **Coliseo Cerrado**

Location Villa El Salvador, Lima

Design and Construction Period 1991 - 1992

Design Team Jorge Burga Bartra and Juan Tokeshi SH.

Structural and Civil Engineering Jorge Alfaro M.

Quantity Surveying and Environmental Engineering Jorge Alfaro +
Partners

Mechanical and Electrical Engineering Jose Alfaro + Partners

Site Area 10,000 m²

Building Area 1,732 m²

Total Floor Area 1,296 m²

Photography Juan Tokeshi, Carlos Cosmopolis, Gabriela Cordova

Peru

Award Likha Award and Gold Medal

Given by UAP The United Architects of the Philippines

Prize Presentation April / 16 / 1995

Members of the Jury Nora Dumlao (chairman), Celia Dizon, Corazon
Tandoc, Janet Gotamco, Ronnie Ver, Elsa Villanueva

Architect **Cesar V. Canchela, Quezon City**

Award Winning Building **NHA - Vitas Medium-Rise Socialized Housing
Project for the Urban Poor**

Location R-10 Vitas, Tondo, Manila, Philippines

Design and Construction Period design: October 1989 - January 1990;
construction: March 1990 - October 1991

Design Team Cesar V. Canchela & Associates, Architects, Interior Design &
Landscape Architecture

Structural and Civil Engineering (Team) Renato R. Ubay, MSCE,
Alcantara-Ubay & Co, R-II Builders Inc.

Quantity Surveying R-II Builders Inc.

Environmental Engineering B & M Engineering

Mechanical and Electrical Engineering Engr. Felipe A. Oliva, Jr., PEE

Interior Design Cesar V. Canchela, Reg. Int. Designer

Landscape Architecture Cesar V. Canchela, Reg. Landscape Architecture

Approximate Cost US$ 8,148,148

Site Area 24,000 m²

Building Area 10,102 m²

Total floor Area 50,150 m²

Photography Cesar V. Canchela

Republic of the Philippines

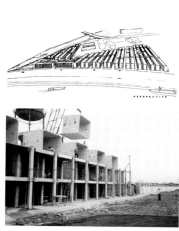

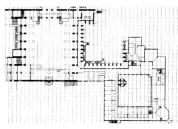

Award SARP Honorary Award for Comprehensive Activities
Given by SARP - Stowarzyszenie Architektów Polskich
Prize Presentation 1993
Architect **Marek Budzyński, Warsaw**
Award Winning Building **The Church of Lord's Ascension**
Location Warsaw
Design and Construction Period 1982 -1992

Design Team Marek Budzyński, Zbigniew Badowski, Piotr Wicha
(concept collaboration)
Structural and Civil Engineering Andrzej Krawczyk, Warsaw
Site Area 0.8 ha
Photography Andrzej A. Mroczek

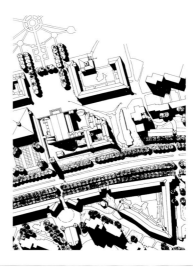

Poland _____

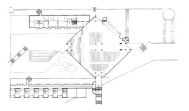

Award Honorary Prize for Comprehensive Activities
Given by SARP - Stowarzyszenie Architektów Polskich
Prize Presentation May / 5 /1994
Members of the Jury Krzysztof Chwalibóg, Szczepan Baum, Marek
Budzyński, Marek Dunikowski, Jerzy Gurawski
Architect **Romuald Loegler, Cracow**
Award Winning Building **The Blessed Jadwigaś Church**
Location Cracow
Design and Construction Period June 1982 - June 1990

Design Team Romuald Loegler and Jacek Czekaj
Structural and Civil Engineering Zdzislaw Trzepla
Mechanical and Electrical Engineering Jan Kwoka, Tadeusz Gasiorek,
Stanislaw Politewicz
Landscape Architecture Romuald Loegler and Jacek Czekaj
Site Area 1.0 ha
Building Area 4,792 m²
Total floor Area 5,927 m²
Photography Romuald Loegler

Poland _____

Award Premio Nacional de Arquitectura
Given by Associação dos Arquitectos Portugueses
Prize Presentation 1993
Architect **Álvaro Siza Vieira, Porto**
Awarded for his Life Work **here: Galician Center of Contemporary Art**
Location Santiago de Compostela, Spain
Design and Construction Period 1988 -1993

Design Team Preliminary project: Joan Falgueras (Architect coordinator),
Mona Trautman (Architect collaboration); Jordi Fossas, Rafael Soto, Angel
Fibla, Joan Genis, Joan Claudi, Joan Claudi Minguel, Jordi Maristany,
Antonio Trilla (Collaboration); Project execution: Yves Stump, João
Sabugueiro (Architect coordinator); Jane Considine, Tiago Faria, Anton Graf,
Cecilia Lau, Elisiário Miranda, Iago Seara Morales (Admin. ass. architect)
Air conditioning Consultants Alfredo Costa Pereira, Paulo Queirós Faria
Engineering Euroconsult
Photography Jeff Goldberg / Esto

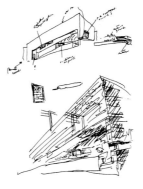

Portugal _____

41

R

Award Yearly Award Union of Romanian Architects

Given by Uniunea Arhitectilor Din Romania (UAR)

Prize Presentation 1992

Members of the Jury Alexandru Sandu, Stefan Lungu, Romeo Belea, U.A.R.

Architects **Constantin Rulea, Mircea Anania, Octav Dimitriu, Dan Ioanovici, Bucharest**

Award Winning Building **Ansamblul Universitar ›LEU‹ (University Complex)**

Location Bucharest, Romania

Design and Construction Period 1974 - 1975

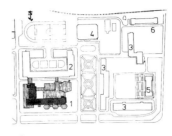
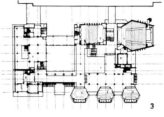
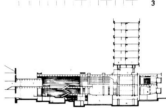

Design Team Constantin Rulea, Mircea Anania, Octav Dimitriu, Dan Ioanovici, Ion Calesanu, Ion Lucacel, Vasile Telea

Structural and Civil Engineering T. Popp, M. Mironescu, S. Gavrilescu, V. Sava, A. Bortnovski, A. Craciun, O. Radu, G. Bratu

Quantity Surveying G. Macuca

Environmental and Electrical Engineering V. Marinescu, A. Bailescu, I. Rosca, D. Scarlatescu, A. Necsulea, N. Wegener, N. Predeleanu, M. Oniga, C. Campeanu, F. Patru, C. Georgescu, A. Vladescu, I. Filimon, I. Ciurec

Interior Design C. Rulea, V. Abraham, A. Popescu, T. Silaghi, R. Matache, C. Visan

Landscape Architecture P. Furtuna, R. Trantz

Approximate Cost US$ 12,000,000

Site Area 30,000 m²

Building Area 3,200 m²

Total Floor Area 24,000 m²

Photography Danila Dumitru

Romania

Award 1- Constantin Joja 1993 / 2- The Major Prize for Architecture in Romania 1994

Given by Uniunea Arhitectilor Din Romania (UAR)

Prize Presentation 1- 1993, 2- 1994

Architect **Serban Sturdza, Timisoara**

Award Winning Building **Expansion of the Children's Hospital to accommodate a Building for Diagnosis and Treatment**

Location Timisoara, Romania

Design and Construction Period 1992 - 1994

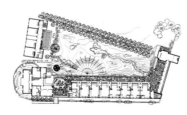
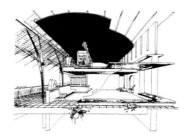

Design Team PRODID Serban Sturdza + Partner

Structural and Civil Engineering PRODID Albert Vallo, M. Gheorghiu

Landscape Architecture PRODID Serban Sturdza, Cameia Covaci

Building Area 3,990 m²

Romania

42

Award First Prize UAR

Given by Union of the Architects of Russia

Prize Presentation September 1994

Members of the Jury V. Egerev, A. Achmedov, V. Davidenko, V. Logvinov
and others

Architect **Mikhail Krishtal, Moscow**

Award Winning Building **Leisure Centre**

Location Durnevo, Kursk Region, Russia

Design and Construction Period 1992 - 1994

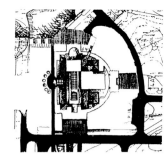

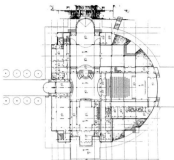

Structural and Civil Engineering Baytur Construction and Contracting Co.
Istanbul, Turkey

Mechanical and Electrical Engineering Baytur Construction and
Contracting Co. Istanbul, Turkey

Interior Design Baytur Construction and Contracting Co. Istanbul, Turkey

Building Area 1,900 m²

Total Floor Area 2,000 m²

Photography M. Krishtal

Russia

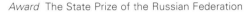

Award The State Prize of the Russian Federation

Given by The President of the Russian Federation

Prize Presentation June 1995

Members of the Jury Russian State Prize Committee

Architects **Yuri Zemtsov, Mikhail Kondiain, Nina Popovskaia, Mikhail**

43 **Baranovsky, Eugeni Barvitsky, St. Petersburg**

Award Winning Building **Nevsky Palace Hotel**

Location Nevsky Prospect 57, St. Petersburg, Russia

Design and Construction Period Design: 1989 - 1990; Construction:
1990 - 1993

Design Team Project: Zemtsov, Kondiain & Partners Architectural Bureau,
St. Petersburg; Executive drawings: Cakman,
Requat & Reinthaller & Partner, Vienna

Structural and Civil Engineering Hermann Kugler, Vienna

Approximate Cost US$ 115,000,000

Site Area 4,870 m²

Building Area 4,870 m²

Total Floor Area 36,351m²

Photography Mikhail Kondiain

Russia

S

Award Prize of Emil Belluš

Given by Society of Slovakian Architects

Slovakia

Prize Presentation 1993

Architect **F. Milučký**

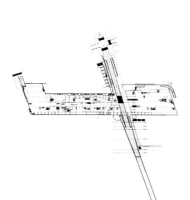
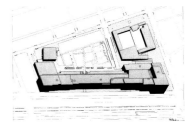

Award Medalla de Oro

Given by Consejo Superior de los Colegios de Arquitectos de España

Prize Presentation 1994

Architect **Miguel Fisac, Madrid**

Award Winning Building **All projects; here: 1- Iglesia Canfranc;
2- Vivienda. Mazarrón; 3- Laboratorios Jorba; 4- Vivienda en
la Moraleja**

Location 1- Huesca; 2- Murcia; 3- Madrid; 4- Madrid, Spain

Design and Construction Period 1- 1963; 2- 1968; 3- 1965; 4- 1973

Spain

Award Premio de la III Bienal de Arquitectura Española ›Manuela de
la Dehesa‹

Given by Ministerio de Obras Públicas, Transportes y Medio Ambiente.
Consejo Superior de los Colegios de Arquitectos de España. Universidad
Internacional Menéndez Pelayc

Prize Presentation July / 20 /1995

Architects **Rafael Moneo/Manuel Solà-Morales, Madrid**

Award Winning Building **L'Illa Diagonal**

Location Barcelona, Spain

Design and Construction Period 1987 -1993

44

Design Team Rafael Moneo and Manuel Solà-Morales; collaboration:
Lluís Tobella, Antón María Pàmies, Andrea Casiraghi, Francesc Santacana,
Lucho Marcial, Félix Wettstein, Román Cisneros, Isabel Pericas,
René Hochuli, Kate Webb, Oriol Mateu

Structural and Civil Engineering Mariano Moneo

Mechanical and Electrical Engineering Sereland, Técnicas Reunidas

Approximate Cost 100,000 Pts/m²

Building Area 180,000 m²

Photography Lluís Casals

Spain

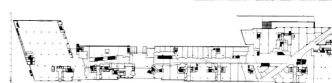

Award 1- Premio Ciutat de Barcelona 1. Premio / 2- Premio Fad
de Arquitectura 1. Premio

Architects **Viaplana / Piñon Arqs. R. Mercadé ASS., Barcelona**

Spain

Award Winning Building **Centro de Cultura Contemporanea,
Casa de Caritat**

Page 170

Award SLIA Design Award

Given by Sri Lanka Institute of Architects (SLIA)

Sri Lanka

Prize Presentation February / 25 / 1995

Architects **Mihindu Keerthiratne Associates Ltd., Colombo**

Award SARs Kasper Salin-Pris

Architects **Rosenbergs Arkitekter AB together with Tekniska Verken
i Linköping AB, Stockholm**

Award Winning Building **Tekniska Verken i Linköping AB**

Sweden

Page 174

Award Auszeichnung für gute Bauten in der Stadt Zürich
Given by Hochbauamt Zürich (on behalf of Schweizerischer Ingenieur-
und Architektenverein)
Prize Presentation 1995
Members of the Jury U. Koch, K. Martelli, H. R. Rüegg, H. Kollhoff,
K. Schattner, P. Zumthor, D. Nievergelt, B. Maeschi, D. Bachmann
Switzerland _____

Architects **ARCOOP: Ueli Marbach, Arthur Rüegg und
Klaus Dolder, Zurich**
Award Winning Building **Villa Bleuler**
Location Zurich, Switzerland

Design Team Thomas von Ballmoos, Monika Stöckli

Award Prix Interassar
Architects **Peter Böcklin, Predrag Petrovic, Geneva**
Award Winning Building **Théâtre de l'Enfance et de la Jeunesse
A. Chavanne**
Switzerland _____

Page 178

Award Auszeichnung für gute Bauten in der Stadt Zürich
Architects **Trix and Robert Haussmann and Steiger Partner,
Architekten und Planer AG, Hansruedi Stierli, Zurich**
Award Winning Building **S-bahn station Museumsstrasse and under-
ground shopping malls**
Switzerland _____

Page 182

Award Auszeichnung für gute Bauten in der Stadt Zürich
Given by Hochbauamt Zürich (on behalf of Schweizerischer Ingenieur-
und Architektenverein)
Prize Presentation 1995
Members of the Jury U. Koch, K. Martelli, H.R. Rüegg, H. Kollhoff,
K. Schattner, P. Zumthor, D. Nievergelt, B. Maeschi, D. Bachmann
Switzerland _____

Architect **Theo Hotz, Zurich**
Award Winning Building **1- Conference Building ›Grünenhof‹ and
2- ›Apollo‹ Building**
Location Zurich, Switzerland

Design Team 1- Heinz Moser, Guido Rigutto und 2- Peter Berger

---

Award Auszeichnung für gute Bauten in der Stadt Zürich
Given by Hochbauamt Zürich (on behalf of Schweizerischer Ingenieur-
und Architektenverein)
Prize Presentation June 1995
Members of the Jury U. Koch, K. Martelli, H.R. Rüegg, H. Kollhoff,
K. Schattner, P. Zumthor
Architects **I+B Architekten, Itten + Brechbühl AG, Zurich**
Award Winning Building **Technopark Zurich**
Location Zurich, Switzerland
Design and Construction Period project: 1985 - 1988, permit: 1989,
construction: 1989 - 1993

Design Team P. Staub, H. Eggen, G. Bölsterli, R. Tropeano, H. Gessler
Structural and Civil Engineering Minikus, Witta, Voss + Partner und Wolf,
Kropf & Zschaber
Environmental Engineering Sulzer Energy Consulting (SEC), Winterthur
Mechanical and Electrical Engineering SEC and Scherler Consulting
Engineering Zurich / Winterthur
Approximate Cost SFr 150,000,000
Site Area 20,000 m²
Building Area 15,000 m²
Total Floor Area 75,000 m² (incl. basement) volume: 315,000 m³
Photography H. Helfenstein, Adliswil, Zurich
Switzerland _____

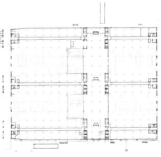

45

Award Auszeichnung für gute Bauten in der Stadt Zürich

Given by Hochbauamt Zürich (on behalf of Schweizerischer Ingenieur-
und Architektenverein)

Prize Presentation 1995

Architects **Kuhn Fischer Partner Architekten AG, Zurich**

Award Winning Building **Brahmshof, enclosure of Brahmsstrasse
in Zurich**

Location Brahmsstrasse 22-24, Zurich, Switzerland

Design and Construction Period 1987 -1991

Design Team Walter Fischer, Collaboration: M. Comte, K. Arn, M. Widmer

Structural and Civil Engineering Jean-Paul Jäger AG, Adliswil

Mechanical and Electrical Engineering Ingenieurbüro Bösch AG,
Unterengstringen; Albrecht + Bolzli, Zurich

Approximate Cost SFr 31,698,000

Site Area 8,353 m²

Building Area 2,885 m²

Total Floor Area 10,144 m²

Photography T. Frey, Eternit

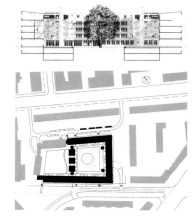

Switzerland

Award Grand Prix Rhénan d'Architecture (Housing)

Given by Association pour le Développement de la Culture et de la
Création Architecturale

Prize Presentation June /13 /1995

Architects **Morger & Degelo Architekten BSA / SIA, Basel**

Award Winning Building **Communal Residence**

Location Müllheimerstrasse 138-140, Basel, Switzerland

Design and Construction Period June 1991 - July 1993

Design Team Morger & Degelo Architekten

Structural and Civil Engineering Gruner AG, Basel

Quantity Surveying Morger & Degelo

Environmental Engineering Gruneco AG, Basel

Mechanical and Electrical Engineering Bretscher AG, Basel

Interior Design Morger & Degelo

Landscape Architecture Morger & Degelo

Approximate Cost SFr 9,498.543

Site Area 1,806 m²

Building Area 812 m²

Total Floor Area 6,008 m²

Photography Ruedi Walti, Basel

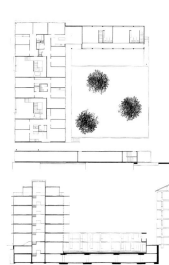

Switzerland

Award Auszeichnung für gute Bauten in der Stadt Zürich

Given by Hochbauamt Zürich (on behalf of Schweizerischer Ingenieur-
und Architektenverein)

Prize Presentation 1995

Members of the Jury U. Koch, K. Martelli, H.R. Rüegg, H. Kollhoff,

K. Schattner, P. Zumthor, D. Nievergelt, B. Maeschi, D. Bachmann

Architects **Isa Stürm und Urs Wolf, Zurich**

Award Winning Building **Boutique Issey Miyake**

Location Zurich, Switzerland

Switzerland

U

Award Award of the Union of Architects of Ukraine
Given by Union of Architects of Ukraine
Prize Presentation 1993
Architects **Tamara Alexandrowna Dawidenko, Kiev; Elena Dmitrijewna Jaskdowitsch, Kiev; Grischtschenka Alexander Pawlowitsch, Ukraine**

Truskavez; Vera Michailowna, Kiev; Wjatscheslaw Nikolajewitsch Pawljukow; Wassily Fedorowitsch Prisjashnjuk, Kiev; Boris Kusmitsch Romanenko, Kiev; Skop Orest Andrejewitsch, Lvov

---

Award RIBA Regional Architecture Award (Wessex Region)
Given by Royal Institute of British Architects
Prize Presentation 1994
United Kingdom

Architects **Arup Associates, London**
Award Winning Building **Canons House, Bristol**

Award FIBA Regional Architecture Award (North West Region)
Given by Royal Institute of British Architects
Prize Presentation 1994
United Kingdom

Architect **Austin-Smith: Lord, Warrington**
Award Winning Building **Aldham Robards Learning Resource Centre, Liverpool and Manchester Airport Station**

Award RIBA Regional Architecture Award (England, South East Region)
Given by Royal Institute of British Architects
Prize Presentation September 1994
Architect **Elspeth Beard, Godalming**
Award Winning Building **Munstead Water Tower**
Location Godalming, Surrey, UK
Design and Construction Period 6 years

Design Team Elspeth Beard
Structural and Civil Engineering Chris Wise
Interior Design Elspeth Beard
Approximate Cost £ 110,000
Site Area 0.25 acres
Building Area 800 sq. ft.
Total Floor Area 5,000 sq. ft.

United Kingdom

Award RIBA Regional Architecture Award (England, Northern Region)
Given by The Royal Institute of British Architects
Prize Presentation 1994
United Kingdom

Architect **Michael Blee Design**
Award Winning Building **Douai Abbey Church and St Paul's Church Centre**

Award RIBA Regional Architecture Award (England, Northern Region)
Given by Royal Institute of British Architects
Prize Presentation December /1/1994
Members of the Jury RIBA Panel
Architects **Jane Darbyshire and David Kendall Ltd., Newcastle upon Tyne**
Award Winning Building **Bradbury House, Cheshire Home**
Location Crook, County Durham, UK
Design and Construction Period June 1990 - September 1992

Design Team Jane Darbyshire, Anthony Reynolds (J.D.K.)
United Kingdom

Structural and Civil Engineering Phil Skinner (Hutter, Jennings & Titchmarsh)
Quantity Surveying RNJ Partnership
Mechanical and Electrical Engineering CWS Engineering Group
Interior Design Alison Thornton (J.D.K.)
Landscape Architecture Elizabeth Kendrick (Kendrick Associates, Keighley)
Approximate Cost £ 1,532,826
Site Area 6,428 m²
Building Area 1,893 m²
Total Floor Area 2,051 m²
Photography Sally Ann Norman, Newcastle Upon Tyne

Award RIBA Regional Architecture Award, 1- Eastern Region ; 2- Scotland
Prize Presentation 1994
Given by Royal Institute of British Architects
United Kingdom

Architects **Jeremy Dixson and Edward Jones, London**
Award Winning Building **1- Darwin Study Centre, Cambridge and
2- Round Tower House & Square Tower House, Aberdeen**

Award RIBA Regional Architecture Award (South West Region)
Given by Royal Institute of British Architects
Prize Presentation 1994
United Kingdom

Architects **Evans & Shalev Architects, London**
Award Winning Building **Tate Gallery, St Ives**

Award RIBA Regional Architecture Award (England, Northern Region)
Given by Royal Institute of British Architects
Prize Presentation 1994
Architects **FaulknerBrowns, Newcastle upon Tyne**
Award Winning Building **Horsley Laboratory**

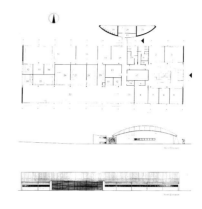

United Kingdom

Award RIBA Regional Architecture Award (Wessex Region)
Given by Royal Institute of British Architects
Prize Presentation 1994
United Kingdom

Architect **Feilden Clegg Design, Bath**
Award Winning Building **Lantern Community Centre, Ringwood and John
Cabot Ctc., Bristol**

Award RIBA Regional Architecture Award (England, South West Region)
Given by Royal Institute of British Architects
Prize Presentation December 1994
Members of the Jury John McAslan (Chairman), Mike Bradbury
Architects **Ferguson Mann Architects, Bristol**
Award Winning Building **Rosemoor Visitors Centre for the Royal
Horticultural Society**
Location Devon, England, UK
Design and Construction Period phase I August 1989 - June 1990,
phase II October 1993 - March 1994

Design Team George Ferguson (RIBA), David Caird (RIBA), David Newton
(ABIAT), Peggy Rickaby (RIBA)
United Kingdom

Structural and Civil Engineering Acer consultants: Hew Owen, Tien Po Tè,
Duncan Leather, Neil Lancaster
Quantity Surveying Messrs Gleeds, London
Environmental Engineering John Willoughby, Gloucester
Mechanical and Electrical Engineering LA Bawden, Gloucester
Interior Design Ferguson Mann Architects
Landscape Architecture Elizabeth Banks Associates, London
Approximate Cost £ 855,000 (including immediate external works,
£ 100,000)
Site Area 7,650 m²
Building Area 835 m²
Total Floor Area 880 m²

Award RIBA Regional Architecture Award (Eastern Region)
Given by Royal Institute of British Architects
Prize Presentation 1994
United Kingdom

Architects **Stephen Greenberg & Dean Hawkes, Cambridge**
Award Winning Building **Principal's Lodge, Cambridge and Friary, Essex**

Award RIBA Regional Architecture Award (England, South West Region)
Architects **Nicholas Grimshaw & Partners Ltd., London**
Award Winning Building **Western Morning News Headquarters & Print
Works, Plymouth**
United Kingdom

Page 186

Award RIBA Regional Architecture Award (England, London Region)
Given by Royal Institute of British Architects
Prize Presentation 1994
Architects **Nicholas Grimshaw & Partners Ltd, London**
Award Winning Building **Waterloo International Terminal**
Location London, UK
Design and Construction Period 1988 - May 1993

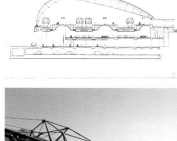

Design Team Nicholas Grimshaw & Partners: Nicholas Grimshaw,
Rowena Bate, Ingrid Bille, Conal Campbell, Garry Colligan, Geoff Crowe,
Florian Eames, Alex Fergusson, Sarah Hare, Eric Jaffres, Ursula Heinemann,
Doug Keys, David Kirkland, Chris Lee, Colin Leisk, Jan Mackie, Julian
Maynard, Neven Sidor, Ulriche Seifutz, Will Stevens, George Stowell,
Andrew Whalley, Robert Wood, Sara Yabsley, Richard Walker, Dean Wyllie,
Paul Fear, Steve McGuckin
Structural Engineering YRM Anthony Hunt Associates (roof and glazing);
Cass Hayward & Partners with Tony Gee & Partners (terminal viaduct);
British Rail Network Civil Engineer (approaches viaduct); Sir Alexander Gibb
& Partners (basement and external works)
Quantity Surveying Davis Langdon & Everest
Mechanical and Electrical Engineering J. Roger Preston & Partners
Approximate Cost £ 130,000,000
Site Area 60,000 m²
Photography Jo Reid and John Peck

United Kingdom _____

Award RIBA Regional Architecture Award (England, Southern Region)
Given by Royal Institute of British Architects
Prize Presentation 1995
Architects **Hampshire County Architects Department, Winchester**
Award Winning Building **The Hampshire County Record Office**
Location Winchester, Hampshire, UK
Design and Construction Period 19 months

Design Team Sir Colin Stansfield Smith (County Architect), Stephen Clow,
David Morriss, Colin Jackson, Julian Gitsham
Approximate Cost £ 5,000,000
Site Area 2 areas
Building Area 2,500 m²
Total Floor Area 2,500 m²

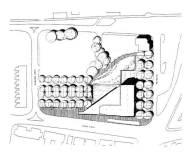

United Kingdom _____

Award RIBA Regional Architecture Award (North West Region)   *Architects* **Hodder Associates, Manchester**
Given by Royal Institute of British Architects   *Award Winning Building* **Oswald Medical Practice, Manchester**
Prize Presentation 1994

United Kingdom _____

United Kingdom

Award RIBA Regional Architecture Award (England, South East Region) *Page* 190
Architects **Michael Hopkins & Partners, London**
Award Winning Building **Glyndebourne Opera House**
United Kingdom

Award RIBA Regional Architecture Award
Given by Royal Institute of British Architects
Prize Presentation November 1995
Architect **MacCormac Jamieson Prichard, London**
Award Winning Building **The Garden Quadrangle, St. John's College**
Location Oxford, UK
Design and Construction Period 1990 -1993 (construction 1991 -1993)

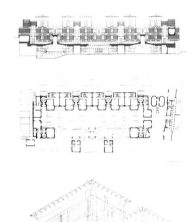

Design Team St. Coomber, N. Dodd, J. Estop, M. Evans,
P. Jamieson, T. Johnson, R. Langheit, A. Lanham, E. Latimer, J. Lewis,
P. Liddell, A. Llowarch, R. MacCormac, J. Paul, Chr. Uhl, J. Wood
Structural and Civil Engineering Price and Myers
Quantity Surveying Northcroft Neighbour & Nicholson
Mechanical, Electrical and Environmental Engineering The Steensen,
Varming and Mulcahy Partnership
Landscape Architecture Judy Astor
Approximate Cost £ 7,500,000
Site Area 2,600 m²
Building Area 1,600 m² footprint
Total Floor Area 3,500 m²

50

Photography Peter Durant / Peter Cook, Alex Beleschenko

United Kingdom

Award 1- Building of the Year 1994 / 2- RIBA National Award / 3- RIBA
Regional Architecture Award (England, West Midlands Region)
Given by 1- Royal Fine Art Commission / Sunday Times, 2- / 3- Royal
Institute of British Architects
Prize Presentation 1- May 1994; 2- / 3- June 1994
Members of the Jury 1- Lord St. John Fawsley, Eva Jaricna
Architect **MacCormac Jamieson Prichard, London**
Award Winning Building **The Cable and Wireless College**
Location Coventry, UK
Design and Construction Period October 1991 - September 1993

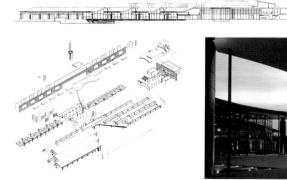

Design Team R. MacCormac and D. Prichard (Partners); St. Cherry
(Associate), D. Wiszniewsk , D. Whitehead, P. Sandhu, S. Mortimer,
S. Usher, K. Whitworth, R. Langheit, A. Llowarch, J. Langford, O. Chapman,
Chr. Bennett, P. Liddell, D. Franklin, H. Brunskill; A. Burns (Administration)
Structural, Mechanical & Electrical Engineering Ove Arup & Partners
Acoustic and Communications Ove Arup & Partners
Quantity Surveying Northcroft Neighbour & Nicholson
Environmental Engineering Ove Arup & Partners
Landscape Architecture Colvin & Moggridge
Approximate Cost £ 20,000,000
Site Area 10 acres
Building Area 12,300 m²
Total Floor Area 12,300 m²

Photography Peter Cook, Robert Fraser
United Kingdom

Award RIBA Regional Architecture Award and RIAI Regional Award (Northern Ireland)
Given by Royal Institute of British Architects and Royal Institute of the Architects of Ireland
Prize Presentation 1994
Architects **McAdam Design, Architects & Civil Engineering , Newtownards**
Award Winning Building **Navan Visitor Centre**
Location Killylea Road, Armagh, Co. Armagh, N.Ireland, UK
Design and Construction Period 2 years

Design Team J. Crothers (Partner in charge), M. Keenan, E. McAdam
Structural and Civil Engineering Cecil Swinton, Bernard Owens
Quantity Surveying W.H. Stephens and Sons
Environmental Engineering Caldwell Partnership
Mechanical and Electrical Engineering Caldwell Partnership
Interior Design McAdam Design / Ideas of York
Landscape Architecture Burns Stewart Partnership
Approximate Cost £ 1,500,000
Site Area 7 ha
Building Area 1,500 m²
Total Floor Area 1,800 m²

United Kingdom

Award RIBA Regional Architecture Award (Scotland)
Given by Royal Institute of British Architects
Prize Presentation December 1994
Architects **McNeish Design Partnership, Motherwell**
Award Winning Building **Bothwell Evangelical Church**
Location Bothwell, Scotland, UK

Design Team Grant Robertson (Project architect)
Structural and Civil Engineering John Allen Associates, Glasgow
Quantity Surveying Muirheads Beard Dove, Glasgow
Acoustic Engineering Sound LAB
Design and Construction Period November 1991 - June 1993
Approximate Cost £ 152,000
Site Area 750 m²
Total Floor Area 182 m² (new building only)
Photography David Cadzow, Grant Robertson

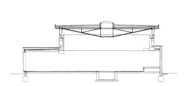

United Kingdom

Award RIBA Regional Architecture Award (England, Eastern Region) and National Award
Given by Royal Institute of British Architects
Prize Presentation 1995
Members of the Jury RIBA - President: D. F. Duffy
Architects **John Miller + Partners Architects, London**
Award Winning Building **The Queen's Building**
Location University of East Anglia, Norwich, UK
Design and Construction Period 1992 -1994

Design Team John Miller + Partners (Partners in charge: John Miller and Richard Brearly)
Structural and Civil Engineering F. J. Samuely and Partners
Quantity Surveying Stockings and Clarke
Environmental Engineering Halcrow Gilbert and Fulcrum Engineering
Mechanical and Electrical Engineering Fulcrum Engineering
Interior Design John Miller + Partners
Landscape Architecture University of East Anglia Grounds Department
Approximate Cost £ 3,300,000
Site Area 1 ha
Building Area 0.5 ha
Total Floor Area 3,500 m²
Photography Dennis Gilbert

United Kingdom

Award RIBA Regional Architecture Award (England, North West Region)
Given by Royal Institute of British Architects
Prize Presentation November 1994
Architects **Mills Beaumont Leavey Channon, Manchester**
Award Winning Building **Library & Learning Resources Centre**
Location Metropolitan University, Chorlton Street, Manchester, UK
Design and Construction Period September 1992 - January 1994

Design Team George Mills, Chris Channon, Andy Avery
Structural and Civil Engineering Les Postawa of Anthony Hunt Associates
Quantity Surveying Appleyard & Trew
Mechanical and Electrical Engineering Preston Lee Chambers
Interior Design Mills Beaumont Leavey Channon & Les Maden
Approximate Cost £ 3,800,000
Site Area 0.168 ha
Building Area 780 m2
Total Floor Area 3,800 m2
Photography Geoff Birch

United Kingdom

Award 1- RIBA Regional Architecture Award (Scotland) / 2- EAA Building
of the Year 1993
Given by 1- Royal Insitute of British Architects; 2- EAA
Prize Presentation 1- 1994; 2- 1993
Architects **Richard Murphy Architects, Edinburgh**
Award Winning Building **Fruitmarket Gallery, Edinburgh**
Location Old Town, Edinburgh, UK
Design and Construction Period 8 months

Design Team Richard Murphy, Graeme Montgomery, Clive Albert,
Lee Hallman, Andrew Byrne
Structural Engineering W. A Fairhursts
Quantity Surveying Ross & Morton
Mechanical and Electrical Engineering W. A. Fairhursts
Approximate Cost £ 350,000
Site Area 420 m2
Building Area 420 m2
Total Floor Area 840 m2
Photography Peter Cook, Alan Forbes

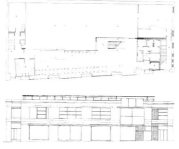

United Kingdom

Award RIBA Regional Architecture Award (Scotland)

Given by Royal Institute of British Architects

Prize Presentation 1994

Architects **Nicoll Russell Studios, Dundee**

Award Winning Building **Scrimgeour's Corner: Housing for Servite**
Housing Association (Scotland) Ltd

Location Comrie Street / West High Street, Crieff, Perthshire, UK

Design and Construction Period appointment of Nicoll Russell Studios:
1988; construction commenced: November 1990; completion of contract:
August 1992

Design Team Nicoll Russell Studios - Partners in charge: R. W. L. Russell,
D. W. Binnie, assisted by: Paul Smith, Bert Barnett, Bill Goodfellow, George
Masson, David Hetherington, Darren Walton

Structural Engineering WA Fairhurst + Partners, Partner in charge:
K. Smith, Project engineer: Donald Fraser

Quantity Surveying Burchell & Partners, Partner in charge: J. E. Kidd,
Project surveyor: Ken McGregor

Mechanical and Electrical Engineering David Elder & Partners: R. Hopkins,
A. Munro

Interior Design Nicoll Russell Studios

Approximate Cost £ 850,000

Site Area 467 m²

Total Building Area 1,640 m²

Area per Floor 328 m²

53

United Kingdom _____

Award RIBA Regional Architecture Award (Wales)

Given by Royal Institute of British Architects

Prize Presentation 1994

Architects **Niall Phillips Architects Ltd, Bristol**

Award Winning Building **Castell Henllys Educational Centre**

Location Eglwyswrw, Dyfed, Wales

Design and Construction Period 10 months

Design Team Niall Phillips Architects Ltd

Structural and Civil Engineering Whitby and Bird, Bath

Quantity Surveying Wheeler Group Consultancy

Environmental Engineering Whitby and Bird

Approximate Cost £ 320,000 (including external works)

Building Area 250 m²

Photography Charlotte Wood

United Kingdom _____

Award RIBA Regional Architecture Award (Wales)

Architects **Niall Phillips Architects Ltd, Bristol**

United Kingdom _____

Award Winning Building **The Welsh Wildlife Centre**

Page 194

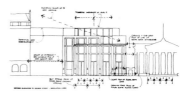

Award RIBA Regional Architecture Award (Scotland)

Given by Royal Institute of British Architects

Prize Presentation 1994

Architects **Reiach & Hall Architects, Edinburgh**

Award Winning Building **Speculative Office Building for the Life Association of Scotland**

Location 10 George Street, Edinburgh, UK

Design and Construction Period 1989 - 1992

Design Team Reiach & Hall Architects

Structural and Civil Engineering Blyth and Blyth

Quantity Surveying Thomson Bethune

Environmental Engineering Blyth and Blyth

Mechanical and Electrical Engineering Blyth and Blyth

Interior Design Reiach & Hall Architects

Approximate Cost £ 10,000,000

Site Area 1,100 m2

Building Area 1,100 m2

Total Floor Area 5,800 m2 (nett)

Photography Alan Forbes

United Kingdom

Award RIBA Regional Architecture Award (England, Southern Region)

Architects **RHWL, Whitby & Bird (for bridge)**

United Kingdom

Award Winning Building **The Anvil, Basingstoke**

Page 198

Page 198

54

Award RIBA Regional Architecture Award (1- East Midlands Region, 2- London Region)

Given by Royal Institute of British Architects

Prize Presentation 1994

United Kingdom

Architects **Rick Mather Architects, London**

Award Winning Building **1- Constable Terrace, Norwich and 2- all Glass Extension, London**

Award RIBA Regional Architecture Award (West Midlands Region)

Given by Royal Institute of British Architects

Prize Presentation 1994

United Kingdom

Architect **Stanton Williams, London**

Award Winning Building **Gas Hall, Birmingham Museums + Art Gallery, Birmingham**

Award RIBA Regional Architecture Award (England, South East Region)

Given by Royal Institute of British Architects

Prize Presentation 1994

Architect **Tibbalds Monro, London**

Award Winning Building **Croydon Library Complex ›The Croydon Clocktower‹**

Location Katharine Street, Croydon, UK

Design and Construction Period 1987 - 1995

Design Team Tibbalds Monro, Chris Colbourne, Michael Patrick

Structural Engineering Michael Barclay Partnership

Services Engineering WSP Kenchington Ford

Quantity Surveying Michael Edwards & Associates

Mechanical and Electrical Engineering Haden Young; Hall Electrical

Approximate Cost £ 30,000,000

Floor Area 6,130 m2

Photography Peter Cook, Lorenzo Elbaz, Michael Patrick

United Kingdom

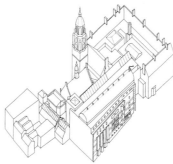

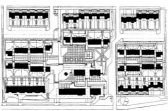

Award Concurso Obra Realizada. Periodo 1982-1992. 1er Premio.
Vivienda Colectiva Urbana

Given by Sociedad de Arquitectos del Uruguay

Prize Presentation November 1992

Members of the Jury H. A. Odriobola, J. Scheps, L. Pimentel,
R. Monteagudo, A. de Betolaza

Architects **H. Aralina, J. Couriel, A. Gravino, M. Spollanzani,
Montevideo**

Award Winning Building **Conjunto Habitacional Barrio Norte**

Location Ciudad Haldomado, Uruguay

Design and Construction Period 1980 - 1985

Structural and Civil Engineering Benjamin Nahoun

Quantity Surveying A. Unahian

Site Area 86,000 m^2

Building Area 5,200 m^2

Total Floor Area 15,000 m^2

Photography H. Spollanzani

Uruguay

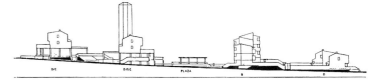

Award Concurso Publico de Obra Realizada: Best Work in the Last
12 Years (1983 - 1995)

Given by Uruguaian Architects Association

Prize Presentation 1995

Members of the Jury Eduardo Folco, Juan Carlos Vanini, Salvador Schelotto

Architects **Ricardo Guguich, Angela Perdomo, Andres Rubilar,
Montevideo**

Award Winning Building **Family House**

Location Pedro Berro No. 742, Montevideo, Uruguay

Design and Construction Period March - December 1992

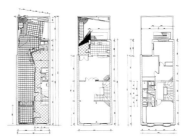

Structural and Civil Engineering Carlos M. Scoseria

Approximate Cost US$ 90,000

Total Floor Area 210 m^2

Photography Ricardo Guguich

Uruguay

Award Concurso Publico de Obra Realizada: Best Work in the Last
12 Years (1983 -1995), Mention

Given by Uruguaian Architects Association

Prize Presentation 1995

Members of the Jury Eduardo Folco, Juan Carlos Vanini, Salvador Schelotto

Architects **Ricardo Guguich, Angela Perdomo, Andres Rubilar,
Montevideo**

Award Winning Building **Banco Santander**

Location 18 de Julio no. 1228, Montevideo, Uruguay

Design and Construction Period 1991 - 1992

Structural and Civil Engineering Carlos M. Scoseria

Mechanical and Electrical Engineering Mario Cabella

Approximate Cost US$ 400,000

Total Floor Area 450 m^2

Photography Ricardo Guguich

Uruguay

Award AIA National Honor Award for Architecture

Given by The American Institute of Architects (AIA)

Prize Presentation 1994

Architects **James Cutler Architects**

USA

Award Winning Building **Salem witch trials tercentenary Memorial**

Location Salem, Massachusetts, USA

Associate Artist Maggie Smith

Award 1- AIA National Honor Award for Architecture / 2- Excellence in
Design Award / 3- Design Award
Architects **Michael Fieldman & Partners, New York**
Award Winning Building **Primary / Intermediate School 217**
USA

Page 202

Award AIA Gold Medal
Architect **Sir Norman Foster, London / Berlin / Frankfurt / Glasgow /
Hong Kong / Tokyo**
USA

Exemplary Work **Stansted Airport**
Page 206

Award AIA National Honor Award for Architecture
Given by The American Institute of Architects (AIA)
Prize Presentation 1994
Architects **Hammond Beeby and Babka Inc., Boston**
Award Winning Building **Paternoster Square Redevelopment
Master Plan**
USA

Location London, UK
Associated Master Planners and Building Architects John Simpson &
Partners, Terry Farrell & Company
Building Design Architects Erith and Terry, Sidell Gibson Partnership, Allan
Greenberg Associates, Demetri Porhyrios Associates, RHWL, Winchester
Design Ltd.

Award AIA National Honor Award for Architecture
Given by The American Institute of Architects (AIA)
Prize Presentation February 1994
Members of the Jury Donlyn Lyndon, Jan Abell, Robert A. Barthelman,
Adele Chatfield-Taylor, Ted Flato, Raymond Gindroz, Magali Sarfatti Larson,
Peter Van Dijk, Betsy West
Architects **Hartman-Cox Architects with Shriver & Holland,
Washington D.C.**
Award Winning Building **The Chrysler Museum**
Location Norfolk, Virginia, USA
Design and Construction Period 1982 - 1989

Structural Engineering James M. Cutts
Mechanical and Electrical Engineering Nash, Love & Associates
Landscape Architecture Peter G. Rolland & Associates
Exhibit Designer Quinrose Design Associates
Lighting Design Claude R. Engle
Approximate Cost US$ 13,000,000
Building Area 50,000 sq. ft. (new Area); 40,800 sq. ft. (remodeled space)
Photography Peter Aaron / ESTO
USA

Award AIA National Honor Award for Architecture
Given by The American Institute of Architects (AIA)
Prize Presentation 1994
Architects **Hellmuth, Obata & Kassabaum, Washington**
USA

Award Winning Building **Oriole Park at Camden Yards**
Location Baltimore, Maryland, USA
Master Plan and Urban Design Hellmuth, Obata & Kassabaum, Sports
Facilities Group, RTKL Associates Inc., Wallace, Roberts & Todd

56

Award AIA National Honor Award for Architecture
Given by The American Insitute of Architects (AIA)
Prize Presentation February 1995
Architects **Ralph Johnson, FAIA/Perry Community Education Village; Perkins & Will, Chicago**
Award Winning Building **Perry Community Education Village**
Location Perry, Ohio, USA

Design and Construction Period Design: June 1991 - August 1993, Construction: August 1993 - August 1995

USA _____

Design Team Perkins & Will, Chicago, Illinois
Structural and Civil Engineering Burgess & Niple, Ltd., Columbus, Ohio
Quantity Surveying CSS Construction Cost System, Inc.
Mechanical and Electrical Engineering Burgess & Niple, Ltd.; Perkins & Will
Landscape Architecture Burgess & Niple
Approximate Cost US$ 91,000,000
Site Area 160 acres
Building Area 500,000 GSF
Total Floor Area 640,000 GSF
Photography Nick Merrick / Hedrich, Blessing Photographers Ltd.

Award AIA National Honor Award for Architecture
Given by The American Institute of Architects (AIA)
Prize Presentation 1994
Architect **Davids Killory**

USA _____

Award Winning Building **Daybreak Grove**
Location Escondido, California, USA

Associate Architect Studio E Architects

Award AIA Honor Award for Excellence in Architectural Design
Given by The American Institute of Architects (AIA)
Prize Presentation February 1994
Members of the Jury Donlyn Lyndon, Jan Abell, Robert Barthelman, Adele Chatfield-Taylor, Ted Flato, Raymond Gindroz, Magali Sarfatti Larson, Peter van Dijk, Betsy West
Architects **R. M. Kliment & Frances Halsband Architects, New York**
Award Winning Building **Computer Science Building, Princeton University**
Location Princeton, New Jersey, USA
Design and Construction Period 1986 - 1989

Design Team R. M. Kliment, F. Halsband, Alejandro Diez, Martin Brandwein, Mark Caligiuri, Mary P. Dowling, Michael A. Nieminen, Karin Robinson
Structural Engineering Robert Silman Associates
Lighting Consultant H. M. Brandston & Partners, Inc.
Mechanical and Electrical Engineering Ambrosino, DePinto & Schmieder, PC
Landscape Architecture Rolland / Towers
Approximate Cost US$ 12,400,000
Building Area 57.000 sq. ft. (new construction)
Photography Cervin Robinson

USA _____

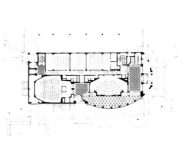

Award AIA National Honor Award for Architecture
Given by The American Institute of Architects (AIA)
Prize Presentation 1994

USA _____

Architects **Koning Eizenberg Architecture Inc., New York**
Award Winning Building **The Simone Hotel**
Location Los Angeles, California, USA

Award The AIA Twenty-Five Year Award
Given by The American Institute of Architects (AIA)
Prize Presentation 1994

USA _____

Architects **Edward Larrabee Barnes / John M. Lee, New York**
Award Winning Building **Haystack Mountain School of Crafts**

57

Award AIA National Honor Award for Architecture

Given by The American Institute of Architects (AIA)

Prize Presentation 1994

Architects **Mockbee / Coker Architects (New York)**

Award Winning Building **Cook Residence**

Location Oxford, Mississippi, USA

Photography Timothy Hursley

USA

Award AIA National Honor Award for Architecture

Given by The American Institute of Architects (AIA)

Prize Presentation 1994

Architects **Pei Cobb Freed & Partners, James Ingo Freed, Design Partner, New York**

Associate Architects **Notter Finegold & Alexander**

Award Winning Building **United States Holocaust Memorial Museum**

Location Washington, D.C., USA

USA

Awards: 1- AIA National Honor Award for Architecture / 2- 1994 Excellence in Design Award from AIA New York State

Architects **Cesar Pelli & Associates, New Haven/Connecticut**

USA

Award Winning Building **Carnegie Hall Tower**

Page 210

58

Award AIA National Honor Award for Architecture

Given by The American Institute of Architects (AIA)

Prize Presentation 1994

Architects **Perkins & Will, Chicago, New York, Berlin**

Award Winning Building **Troy High School**

Location Troy, Michigan, USA

Photography Hedrich, Blessing Photographers Ltd.

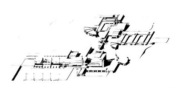

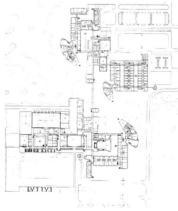

USA

Award AIA National Honor Award for Architecture

Given by The American Institute of Architects (AIA)

Prize Presentation 1994

USA

Architects **Prentice & Chan (Ohlhausen)**

Award Winning Building **The Cooper Union Residence Hall**

Location New York City, New York, USA

Award AIA National Honor Award for Architecture
Given by The American Institute of Architects (AIA)
Prize Presentation February 1994
Architects **William Rawn Associates, Boston**
Award Winning Building **Charlestown Navy Yard Rowhouses**
Location Charlestown, Massachusetts, USA

Design Team William Rawn Associates, Boston
Approximate Cost US$ 67 / sq. ft.
Site Area 0.75 acres

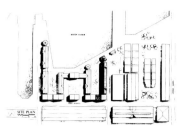
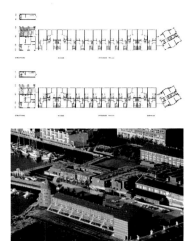

USA

Award AIA National Honor Award for Architecture
Architects **William Rawn Associates, Architects, Inc., Boston**
Award Winning Building **Seiji Ozawa Hall at Tanglewood**
USA

Page 214

Award AIA National Honor Award for Architecture
Given by The American Institute of Architects (AIA)
Prize Presentation 1994
USA

Architects **Ross Barney + Jankowski**
Award Winning Building **César Chavèz Elementary School**
Location Chicago, Illinois, USA

Award AIA National Honor Award for Architecture
Given by The American Institute of Architects (AIA)
Prize Presentation 1994
USA

Architects **Schwartz / Silver Architects Inc.**
Award Winning Building **Firehouse Civic Center**
Location Newburyport, Massachusetts, USA

Award AIA National Honor Award for Architecture
Given by The American Institute of Architects (AIA)
Prize Presentation 1994
USA

Architects **Skidmore, Owings & Merrill, New York**
Award Winning Building **Rowes Wharf**
Location Boston, Massachusetts, USA

Award AIA National Honor Award for Architecture
Architects **Tanner Leddy Maytum Stacy Architects, San Francisco**
Award Winning Building **Corson-Heinser Live / Work**
USA

Page 218

Z

Award Tri-annual Award
Given by Zambia Institute of Architects
Zambia

Prize Presentation June / 30 /1995
Architects **Anderson & Anderson International, Lusaka**

Award Tri-annual Award in Category of Commercial
Given by Zambia Institute of Architects
Prize Presentation June / 30 , 1995
Members of the Jury David Smail
Architects **Lisulo, Malenga & Bwalya - Architects, Lusaka**
Award Winning Building **Rural Bank Building for the Zambia National Commercial Bank**
Location Mkushi Town, Zambia
Design and Construction Period 2 years

Structural and Civil Engineering Muyuni and Partners
Quantity Surveying Mwitumwa and Associates
Mechanical and Electrical Engineering North Atlantic Engineering Consultants
Interior Design Lisulo, Malenga and Bwalya - Architects
Landscape Architecture Lisulo, Malenga and Bwalya - Architects
Approximate Cost US$ 400,000
Site Area 4,732 m²
Building Area 650 m²
Total Floor Area 650 m²
Photography Lisulo, Malenga and Bwalya - Architects
Zambia

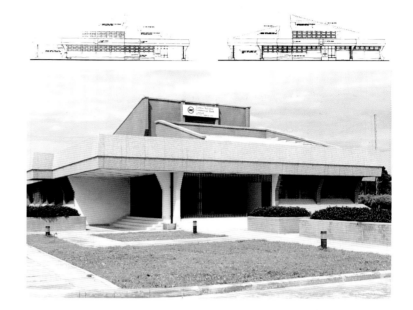

Award Award of Merit
Given by Institute of Architects of Zimbabwe
Prize Presentation February 1995
Architects **Architects Design Group, Harare**
Award Winning Building **Studio Lever, Helensvale**
Location Harare, Zimbabwe

Design and Construction Period 18 months
Approximate Cost Zim$ 235,000

Zimbabwe

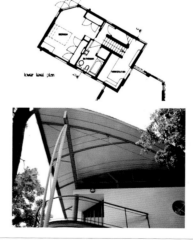

Award Award of Merit
Given by Institute of Architects of Zimbabwe
Prize Presentation October 1994
Members of the Jury Herbert Prins, Peter Oldfield, Sam Naggo, Eva Gurney, Geoff Brakspear
Architects **Julian Conrad Architects, Harare**
Award Winning Building **Finsure House**
Location Corner Union Ave., 2nd Street, Harare, Zimbabwe

Design Team Julian Conrad, Jero Young, Roger Sheard
Structural and Civil Engineering Cresswell Associates
Quantity Surveying Turner & Townsend, Africa
Mechanical and Electrical Engineering Stewart Scott
Interior Design Michelle Conrad
Approximate Cost Zim$ 65,000,000
Site Area 1,680 m²
Building Area 1,428 m²
Total Floor Area 9,978 m²

Zimbabwe

Award Award of Excellence

Given by Institute of Architects of Zimbabwe

Prize Presentation February / 21 / 1995

Architects **Fleet Utria Architecture, Harare**

Award Winning Building **House Cohen, Private Residence**

Location Harare, Zimbabwe

Z i m b a b w e

Award National Award for Excellence in Architecture: Certificate of Merit

Given by Institute of Architects of Zimbabwe

Prize Presentation February / 21 / 1995

Members of the Jury P. Oldfield, H. Prins, E. Gurney, S. Naggo,
G. Brakspear

Architects **Hope Mills Peto Associates, Harare**

Award Winning Building **Extension to St. Theresa's Cathedral**

Location Gweru, Zimbabwe

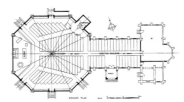

Structural and Civil Engineering Atkinson, Dickie & Partners

Quantity Surveying Paul Harris Associates

Design and Construction Period 1989-1993

Approximate Cost Zim$ 1.35 million

Building Area 470 m2 (additional)

Total Floor Area 470 m2 (additional)

61 **Z i m b a b w e**

Award Award of Excellence

Given by Institute of Architects of Zimbabwe

Prize Presentation February 1995

Architect **Gordon Norman, Bulawayo**

Z i m b a b w e

Award Award of Excellence

Given by Institute of Architects of Zimbabwe

Prize Presentation February 1995

Architect **Pearce Partnership, Harare**

Z i m b a b w e

Award National Architecture Award - Honourable Mention

Given by Institute of Architects of Zimbabwe

Prize Presentation October 1994

Members of the Jury Peter Oldfield, Geoff Brakspear, Herbert Prins

Architect **Graham Price, Harare**

Award Winning Building **Caltex Head Office**

Location Harare, Zimbabwe

Design and Construction Period 2 years

Design Team The Price Ward Wilson Partnership

Structural and Civil Engineering Atkinson & Dickie Partnership

Quantity Surveying Turner & Townsend

Mechanical and Electrical Engineering Merz Scott Wilson Engineering

Interior Design The Price Ward Wilson Partnership

Approximate Cost Zim$ 40,000,000

Site Area 1,200 m2

Building Area 550 m2 (typical floor)

Total Floor Area 4,100 m2

Z i m b a b w e

Award National Architecture Award - Honourable Mention

Given by Institute of Architects of Zimbabwe

Prize Presentation February 1995

Members of the Jury Herbert Prins, Sam Naggo, Eva Gurney,
Peter Oldfield, Geoff Brakspear

Architects **The Stone / Beattie Studio, Harare**

Award Winning Building **United Touring Group - Urban Infill Housing**

Location Victoria Falls

Design and Construction Period 22 months

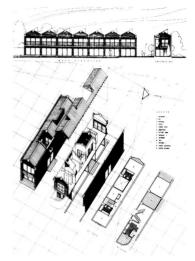

Design Team Richard Beattie Penny Stone

Structural and Civil Engineering Muir Associates - T. Miles, I. Robinson

Quantity Surveying Turner and Townsend Africa

Approximate Cost Zim$ 2,900,000

Site Area 1,400 m²

Building Area 420 m²

Total Floor Area 840 m²

Photography Zambezi Productions

Z i m b a b w e

Award Award of Excellence

Given by Institute of Architects of Zimbabwe

Z i m b a b w e

Prize Presentation February 1995

Architect **Anthony J. Wales-Smith, Harare**

Award Award of Merit

Given by Institute of Architects of Zimbabwe

Prize Presentation October 1994

Members of the Jury Peter Oldfield, Geoff Brakespear, Herbert Prins

Architect **Josh Ward, Harare**

Award Winning Building **Victoria Falls Safari Lodge**

Location Victoria Falls

Design and Construction Period 20 months

Design Team The Price Ward Wilson Partnership

Z i m b a b w e

Structural and Civil Engeneering Atkinson & Dickie, Partnership

Quantity Surveying Corry & Rhodes

Mechanical and Electrical Engineering
Merz Scott Wilson

Interior Design Belinda Jones

Landscape Architecture Grace Gardens

Approximate Cost Zim$ 22,000,000

Site Area 60 ha

Building Area 5,000 m²

Total Floor Area 8,000 m²

DETAILED DESCRIPTIONS OF SELECTED PROJECTS:
A REPRESENTATIVE CROSS-SECTION

Award Robin Boyd Award for Housing
Given by Royal Australian Institute of Architects (RAIA)
Prize Presentation November 1994
Members of the Jury Neville Quarry (Chairperson), James Taylor,
Graham Bligh, Peter Crone, Rebecca Gilling
Architect Bud Brannigan, St. Lucia
Award Winning Building **Brannigan Residence**
Location Brisbane, Australia
Design and Construction Period January - December 1992

Structural and Civil Engineering Les Adsett, Tod Group
Landscape Architecture Donald Irving
Approximate Cost Aus$ 150,000
Site Area 380 m²
Building Area 160 m²
Total Floor Area 220 m²
Photography Adrian Boddy

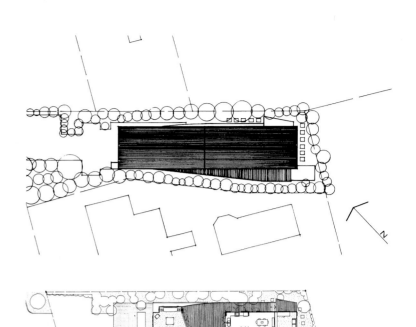

DOWNSTAIRS

A u s t r a l i a
B u d B r a n n i g a n

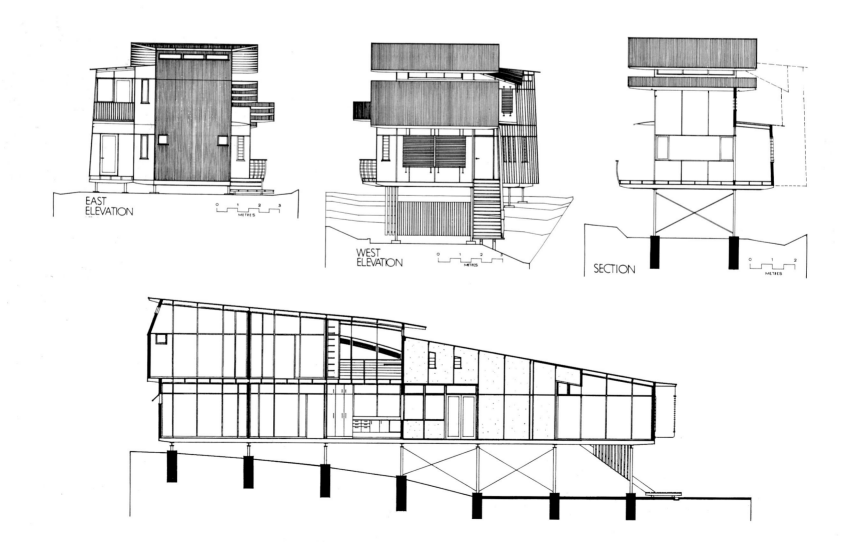

EAST
ELEVATION

WEST
ELEVATION

SECTION

Australia

Award Commercial Architecture Award

Given by Royal Australian Institute of Architects (RAIA)

Prize Presentation November 1994

Members of the Jury Neville Quarry, Peter Crone, Graham Bligh

Architects Guymer Bailey Architects Pty. Ltd., Fortitude Valley

Award Winning Building **Kingfisher Bay Resort and Village (Qld)**

Location Fraser Island, Queensland, Australia

Design and Construction Period 1991 -1992

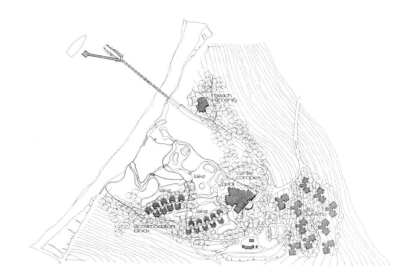

Design Team Tim Guymer, Ralph Bailey, Mark French, Stewart Webb, Bruce Medek, Jim Gall, Margaret Ward, John Blackley, Craig Sargeant, Jola Pietka, Janusz Giermanski

Structural and Civil Engineering Glynn Tucker, Holmes McLeod, Breene and Crane

Quantity Surveying Rider Hunt Australia

Mechanical and Electrical Engineering Bassetts Engineering

Interior Design Guymer Bailey Architects Pty. Ltd.

Landscape Architecture Guymer Bailey Architects Pty. Ltd.

Approximate Cost Aus$ 35,000,000

Site Area 6.5 ha

Building Area 2 ha

Total Floor Area 23,000 m²

Photography Graham Phillip

68   **Australia**

Guymer Bailey Architects

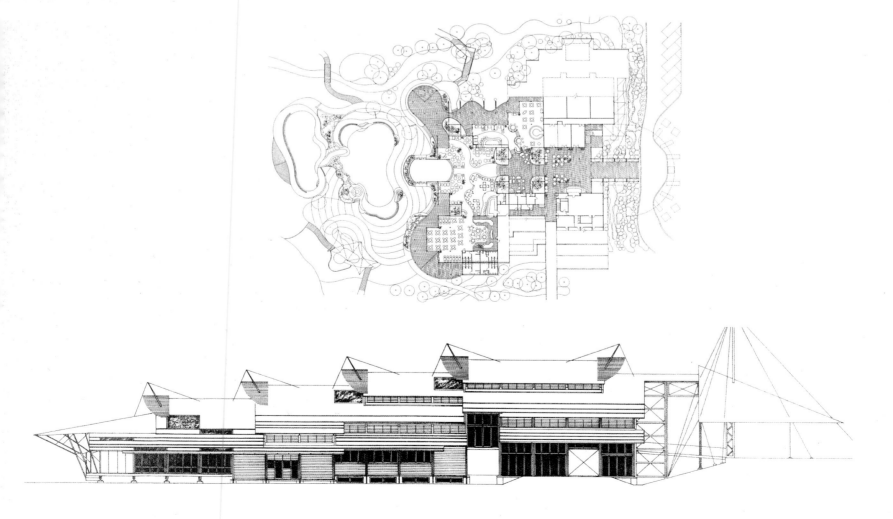

Australia

Award International Award
Given by Royal Australian Institute of Architects (RAIA)
Prize Presentation 1994
Members of the Jury Neville Quarry, Rebecca Gilling, Peter Crone, James
Taylor, Graham Bligh
Architects Kerry Hill Architects (with Akitek Jururancang), Singapore
Award Winning Building **The Datai (Malaysia)**
Location Jalan Teluk Datai, Pulau Langkawi, Kedah, Malaysia
Design and Construction Period August 1989 - November 1993

Design Team Kerry Hill, Wong Mun Summ, Didier Lefort
Structural and Civil Engineering Structural: Rahulan Zain Associates;
Civil: Ranhill Bersekutu
Quantity Surveying Nik Farid & Low
Mechanical and Electrical Engineering Ranhill Bersekutu
Interior Design Lefort Vaichere with Kumpulan Cipta
Landscape Architecture Malik Lip & Associates
Approximate Cost 70,000,000 Malaysian Ringgit (1992)
Site Area 728 ha
Building Area 30,000 m² (includes external areas like pools, etc.)
Photography Albert Lim

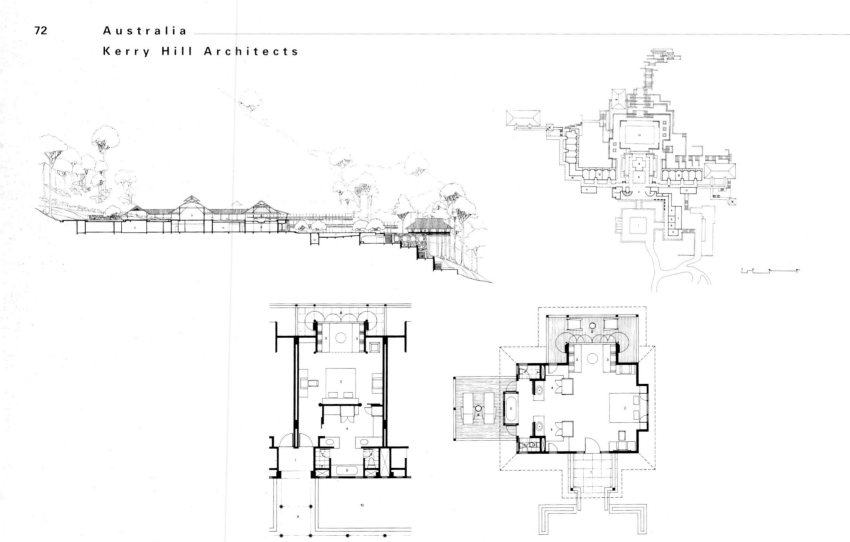

Plan typical guestroom

Plan typical villa

Australia

Award Preis der Zentralvereinigung der Architekten Österreichs
Given by Zentralvereinigung der Architekten Österreichs
Prize Presentation November 1994
Architect THE OFFICE, Vienna
Award Winning Building **Supermarket Merkur**
Location Deutsch Wagram, Austria
Design and Construction Period January 1993 - March 1994

Structural and Civil Engineering Norbert Schmiedehausen
Quantity Surveying Polly
Environmental Engineering ZFG-Projekt
Mechanical and Electrical Engineering Mobiplan-Schmied, Maria Enzersdorf
Interior Design THE OFFICE
Landscape Architecture Irena Rosc
Approximate Cost ÖS 80,000,000
Site Area 14,000 m²
Building Area 3,210 m²
Total Floor Area 3,500 m²
Photography Rupert Steiner, Vienna

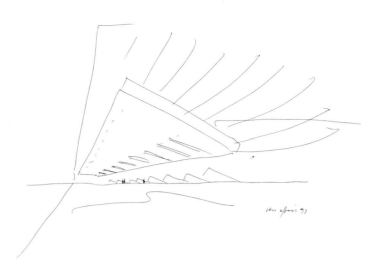

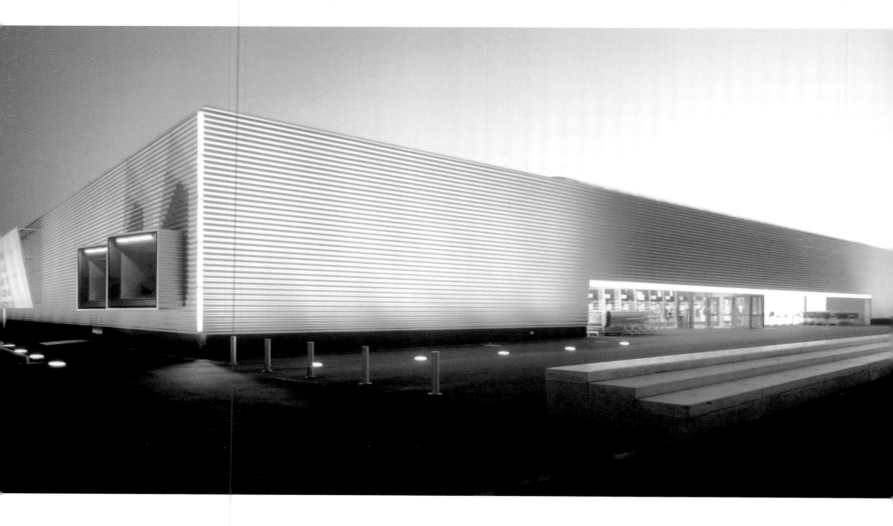

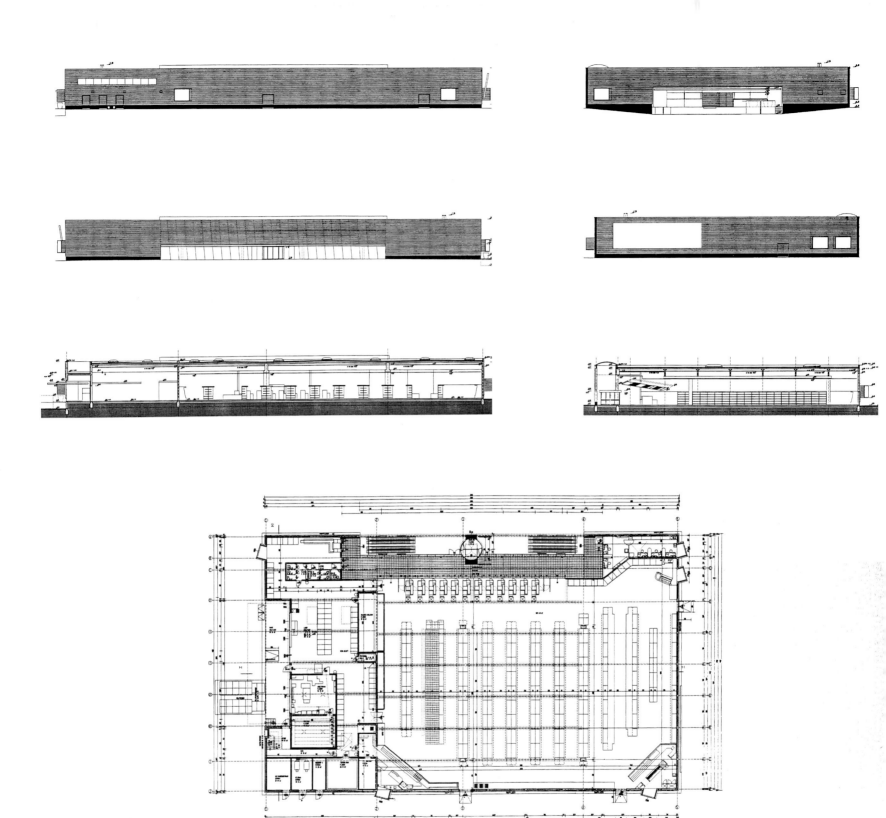
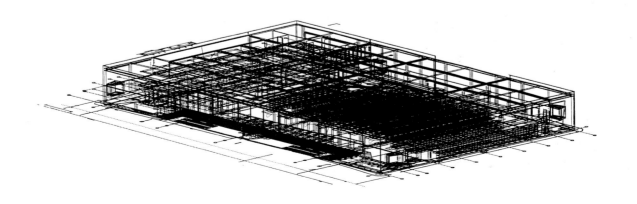

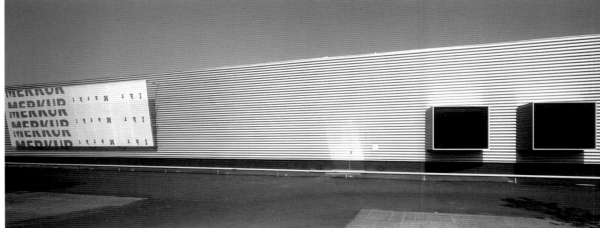

Award Prêmio Habitação / Premiação IAB
Given by Instituto de Arquitetos do Brasil
Prize Presentation March / 22 /1995
Members of the Jury Joaquim Guedes (President), Tito Lívio Frascino,
Gianfranco Vannucchi, Abrahão Sanovicz, Marilia Santana de Almeida, Decio
Tozzi, Willis Myasaka, Fabio Penteado
Architect Carlos Bratke, São Paulo, Brazil
Award Winning Building **Mountain House**
Location Campos do Jordao, São Paulo, Brazil
Design and Construction Period 1992 /1993

Design Team Carlos Bratke, João Belo
Structural and Civil Engineering Aluizio D'Avila Engenheiros
Quantity Surveying Wagner / Engenheiros
Mechanical and Electrical Engineering MHA
Interior Design Carlos Bratke, Denise Barretto
Landscape Architecture Carlos Bratke, Denise Barretto
Approximate Cost US$ 150,000
Site Area 7,000 m²
Building Area 230 m²
Photography José Moscardi Jr., Carolina Bratke

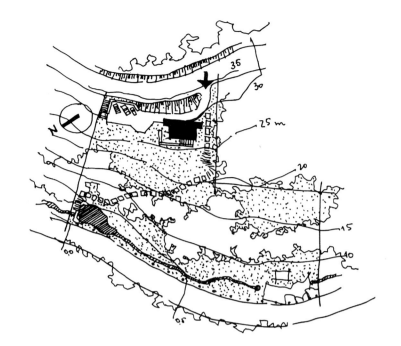

80   **B r a z i l**

C a r l o s   B r a t k e

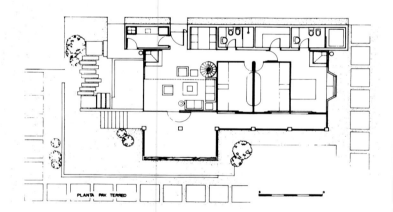

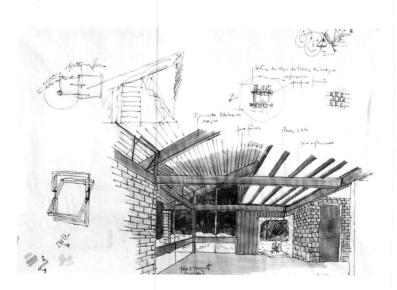

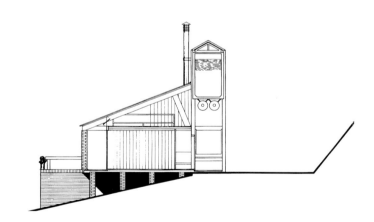

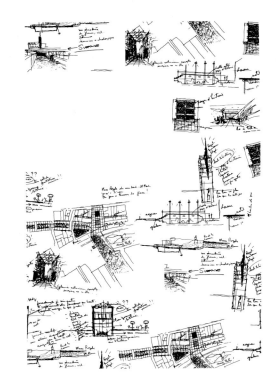

Award Governor General's Award for Architecture
Given by The Royal Architectural Institute of Canada and the Canada
Council
Prize Presentation 1994
Members of the Jury Nigel Baldwin, Essy Baniassad, Odile Hénault,
Raymond Moriyama, Jeremy Sturgess, Billie Tsien
Architects Dan S. Hanganu, Architectes and Provencher Roy, Architectes,
Montréal
Award Winning Building **Pointe-à-Callière, Musée d'Archéologie et
d'Histoire de Montréal**
Location Montréal, Québec, Canada
Design and Construction Period February 1990 - May 1992

Design Team Design: Dan Hanganu (Direction), Thomas Schweitzer,
Luc Plante, Gilles Prud'homme; Technique: Michel Roy (Direction),
Claude Provencher, Alain Desforges, Alain Compéra, Jacques Biard,
François Poirier, Guy Pageau
Structural and Civil Engineering Nicolet Chartrand Knoll Ltée
Mechanical and Electrical Engineering Liboiron Roy Caron + Associés
Approximate Cost Can$ 13,500,000
Total Floor Area 6,935 m²

82 **Canada**

Dan S. Hanganu, Architectes, Provencher Roy, Architectes

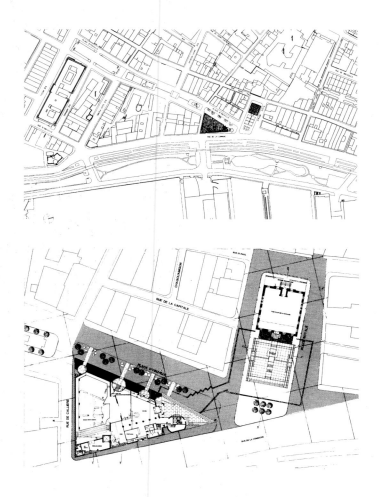

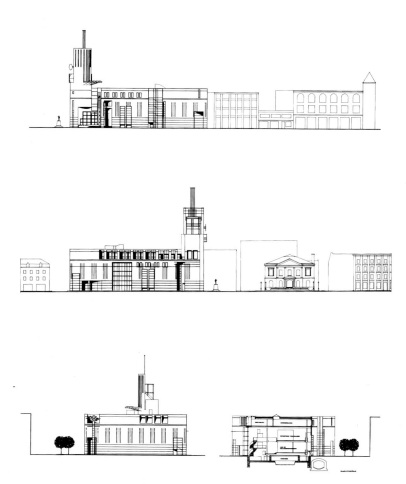

Award Governor General´s Award for Architecture

Given by The Royal Architectural Institute of Canada (RAIC)

Prize Presentation October 1994

Members of the Jury Nigel Baldwin, Essy Baniassad, Odile Hénault,
Ray Moriyama, Jeremy Sturgess, Billie Tsien

Architects Richard Henriquez, Laszlo Nemeth Associates, Architects in
Joint Venture, Vancouver

Award Winning Building **Environmental Sciences Building,
Trent University**

Location Peterborough, Ontario, Canada

Design and Construction Period 1988 -1991

Structural and Civil Engineering Yolles Partnership Inc.

Mechanical and Electrical Engineering Mechanical: The Mitchell
Partnership Inc.; Electrical: Mulvey & Banani International Inc.

Landscape Architecture Cornelia Hahn Oberlander

Approximate Cost Can$ 13,000,000

Building Area 80,000 sq. ft.

Photography Steven Evans

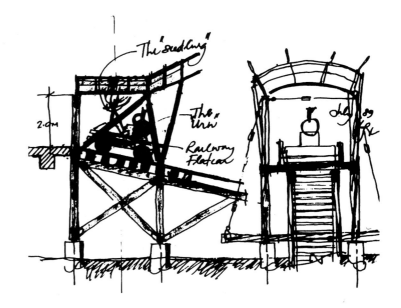

86 **Canada**

Richard Henriquez, Laszlo Nemeth Associates

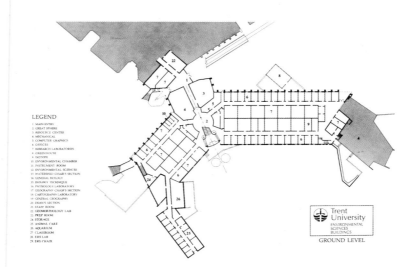

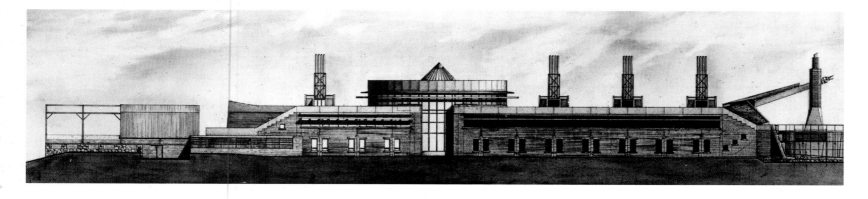

Canada

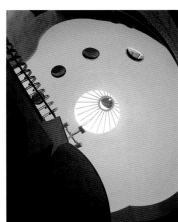

89

Canada

Award Governor General's Award for Architecture
Given by The Royal Architectural Institute of Canada (RAIC)
Prize Presentation 1994
Architects Kuwabara Payne McKenna Blumberg Architects, Toronto
Award Winning Building **Reisman-Jenkinson House and Studio**
Location Richmond Hill, Ontario, Canada
Design and Construction Period 1991

Design Team Bruce Kuwabara, Thomas Payne, Marianne McKenna,
Shirley Blumberg
Structural Engineering M. S. Yolles + Partners
Approximate Cost Can$ 550,000
Photography Steven Evans

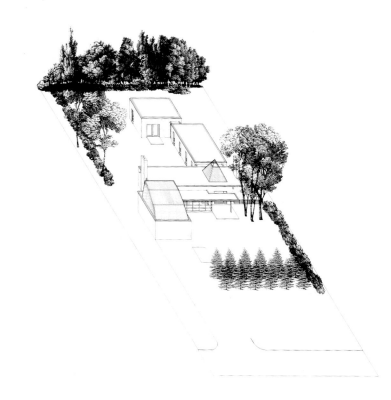

Canada
Kuwabara Payne McKenna Blumberg Architects

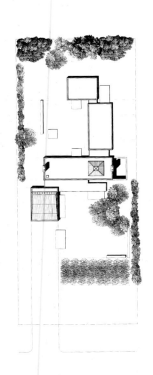

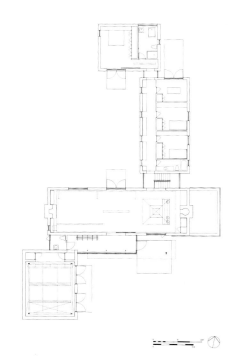

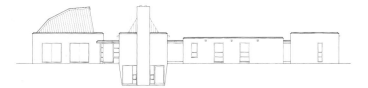

Canada

Award Creation Awards of the Architectural Society of China between the Years
of 1988 - 1992
Given by The Architectural Society of China
Prize Presentation November 1992
Members of the Jury Ye Rutang, Zhou Qinlin, Zhang Zugang, Zhang Qinnan,
Yan Xinhua, Dai Fudong, Peng Yigang, Li Daozeng, Luo Xiaowei
Architect Zhang Jinqiu, Xian
Award Winning Building **Shaanxi Historical Museum**
Location Xian, Shaanxi, P. R. China
Design and Construction Period Design: April 1984 - December 1987;
Construction: July 1987 - June 1991

Design Team Wang Tianxing, Li Zhongzhi, Wang Qi, Wang Shumao, Jiang Enkai
Structural and Civil Engineering Wang Qingxiang, Fan Yuanguan, Tong Yinli
Environmental Engineering Zhao Hanweh, Fu Zen
Mechanical and Electrical Engineering Xu Wengin, Pan Weimin, Hu Yian
Interior Design An Zhifeng
Landscape Architecture Gao Chaojun
Approximate Cost US$ 40,000,000
Site Area 6.5 ha
Building Area 20,530 m²
Total Floor Area 45,800 m²

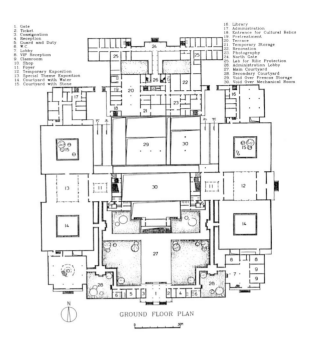

1. Gate
2. Ticket
3. Consignation
4. Reception
5. Guard and Duty
6. W.C.
7. Lobby
8. VIP Reception
9. Classroom
10. Shop
11. Foyer
12. Temporary Exposition
13. Special Theme Exposition
14. Courtyard with Water
15. Courtyard with Stone
16. Library
17. Administration
18. Entrance for Cultural Relics
19. Pretreatment
20. Terrace
21. Temporary Storage
22. Renovation
23. Photography
24. North Gate
25. Lab for Relic Protection
26. Administration Lobby
27. Main Courtyard
28. Secondary Courtyard
29. Void Over Frescos Storage
30. Void Over Mechanical Room

GROUND FLOOR PLAN

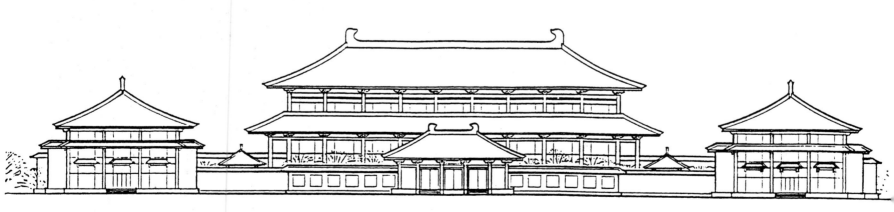

China

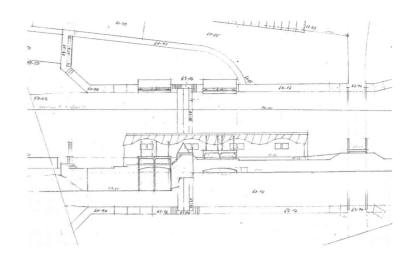

Award Grand Prix of the Association of Czech Architects 1994 and also
a prize in the category of new buildings
Given by The Association of Czech Architects
Prize Presentation 1995
Architect Roman Koucký, Prague
Award Winning Building **Re-cycling Centre with a Sewage Plant,**
Horní Maršov
Location Horní Maršov, Czech Republic
Design and Construction Period 1992 - 1994

Design Team Roman Koucký Architektonická Kancelář
Building Area 207.36 m^2
Photography Ester Havlová and Roman Koucký

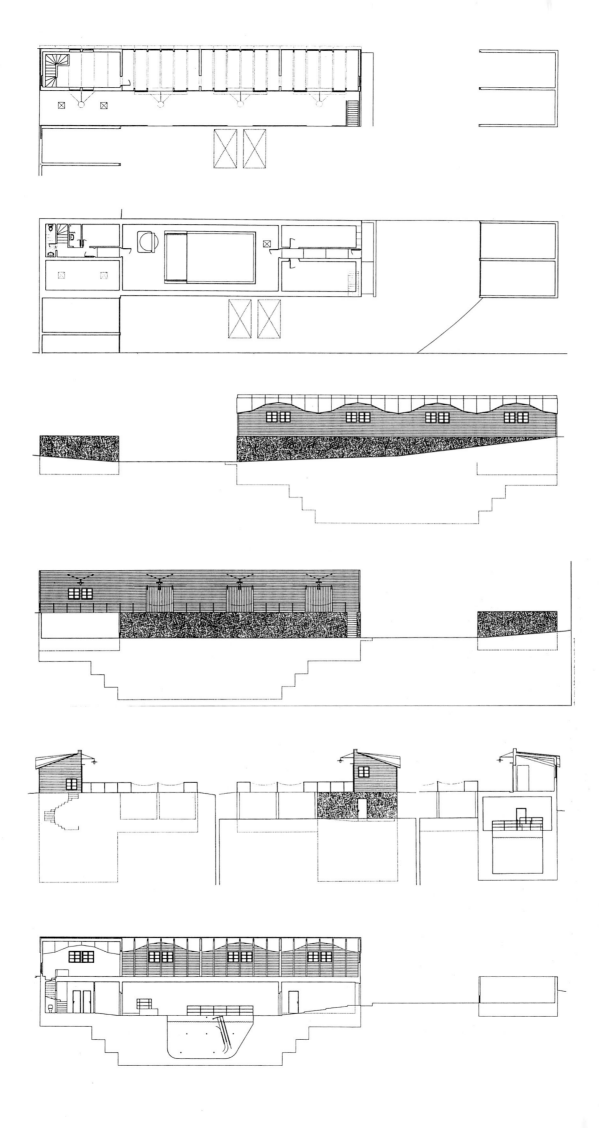

Award Architectural Design Grand Award

Given by Pan-American Biennal of Architecture

Prize Presentation December 1994

Architects Mitchell / Giurgola Architects, in association with Rancorn
Wildman, Krause and Brezinski

Award Winning Building **Virginia Air and Space Center**

Location Hampton, Virginia, USA

Design and Construction Period 1992

Design Team Mitchell / Giurgola Architects (New York), in association with
Rancorn Wildman, Krause and Brezinski

Approximate Cost US$ 18,040,000 (general construction); US$ 4,743,675
(construction cost for garage)

Building Area 118,000 sq. ft. (museum); 171,000 sq. ft. (parking garage)

Photography Jeff Goldberg / Esto

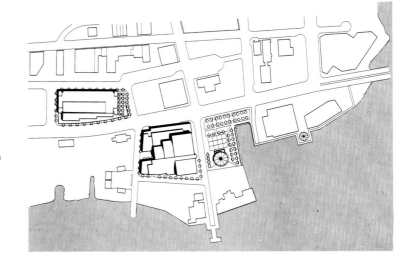

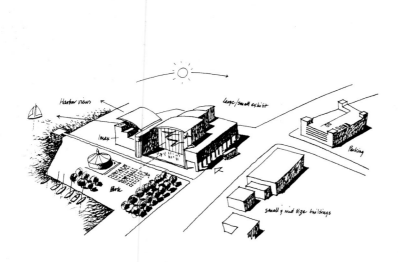

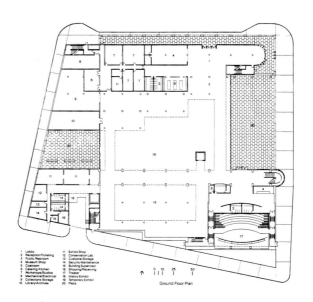

Ground Floor Plan

1 Lobby
2 Reception/Ticketing
3 Public Restroom
4 Museum Shop
5 Coatroom
6 Catering Kitchen
7 Workshops/Studios
8 Mechanical/Electrical
9 Collections Storage
10 Library/Archives
11 Exhibit Shop
12 Conservation Lab
13 Custodial Storage
14 Security Maintenance
15 Building Supervisor
16 Shipping/Receiving
17 Theater
18 History Exhibit
19 Temporary Exhibit
20 Plaza

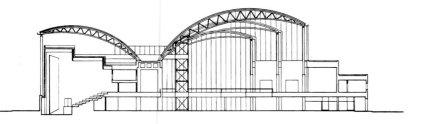

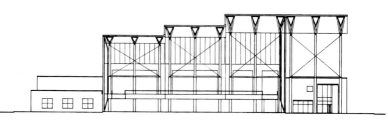

Ecuador

Award Gran Premio Internacional IX Bienal Panamericana de Arquitectura
de Quito
Given by Colegio de Arquitectos del Ecuador
Prize Presentation November /18 /1994
Members of the Jury J. Guedes (Brazil), F. Espinosa (Ecuador), E. Yanes
(Spain), H. de Garay (Venezuela), A. Saldariaga (Colombia), J. Ordoñez
(Ecuador)
Architect Jorge Rigamonti, Caracas, Venezuela
Award Winning Building **Campamento Turístico Cayo Crasquí**
Location Cayo Crasqui, Archipielago Los Roques, Venezuela
Design and Construction Period 1991 - 1994

Design Team Helena Rigamonti, Carmen Marquina, Lino Becerra, Luis Cediel
Structural and Civil Engineering Francisco Niubo Ribo
Environmental Engineering Jose Pojan L.
Mechanical and Electrical Engineering Sergio Popoli
Interior Design Rigamonti & Asociados Consultores
Landscape Architecture Jorge Rigamonti
Approximate Cost US$ 2,000,000
Site Area 30,000 m²
Building Area 1,684 m²
Total Floor Area 2,420 m²
Photography Jorge Rigamonti

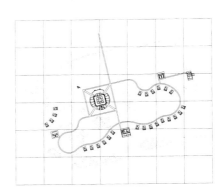

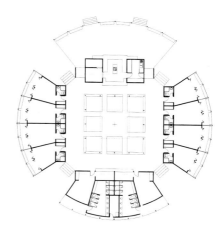

104 E c u a d o r

J o r g e   R i g a m o n t i

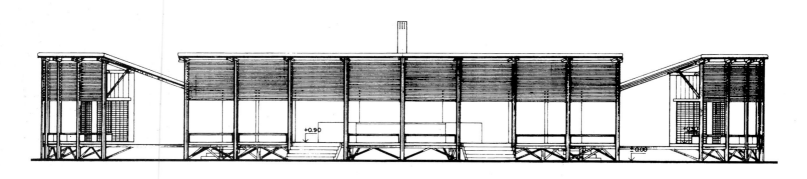

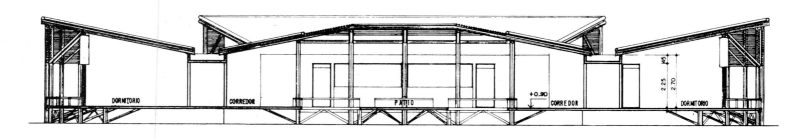

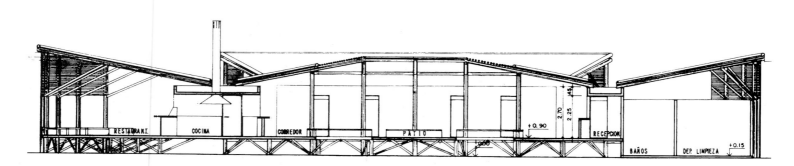

Award 1- Second Prize for Town-Planning / 2- Special Prize of the
›Equerre d'Argent‹
Given by 1- Fondation of the Academy of Architecture / 2- The Journal
Moniteur
Prize Presentation 1- 1990; 2- October 1995
Architect Dominique Perrault, Paris
Award Winning Building **Bibliothèque nationale de Paris**
Location Paris, France
Design and Construction Period 1989 - 1995

Structural and Civil Engineering Perrault Associés SA
Quantity Surveying Pieffet Corbin Tomasina
Mechanical and Electrical Engineering Technip Seri Construction
Interior Design Dominique Perrault, Gaëlle Lauriot Prevost
Approximate Cost FF 3.6 Milliards (exclusive of VAT)
Site Area 80,000 m²
Building Area 80,000 m²
Total Floor Area 350,000 m²
Photography Georges Fessy, Michel Denancé

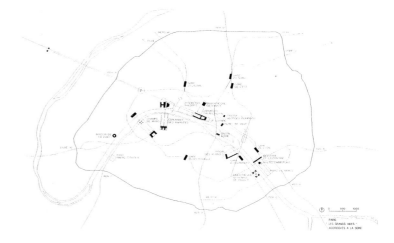

106   **F r a n c e**

D o m i n i q u e   P e r r a u l t

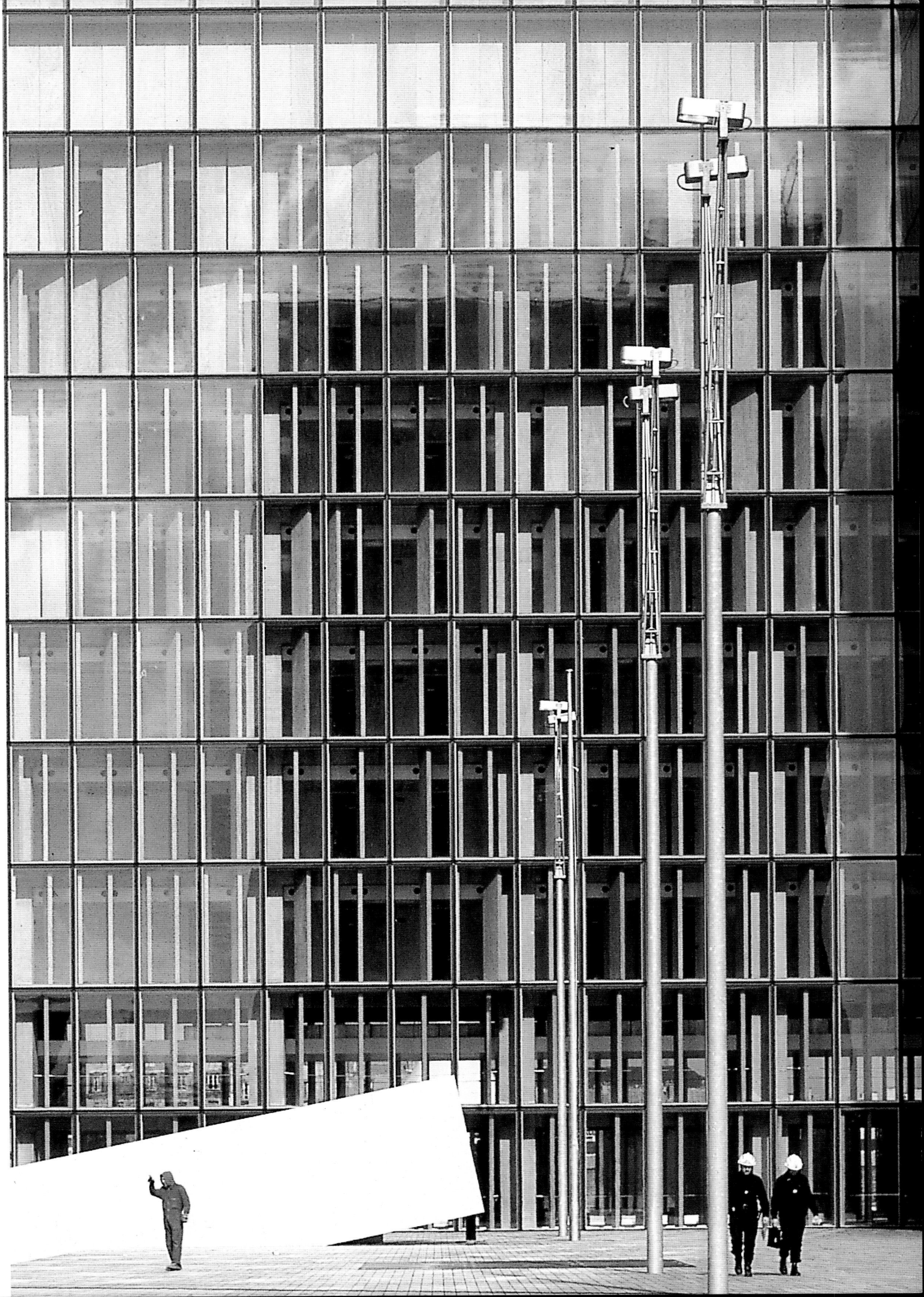

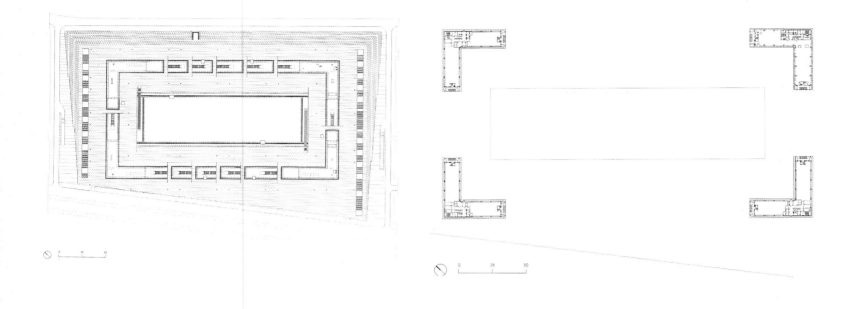

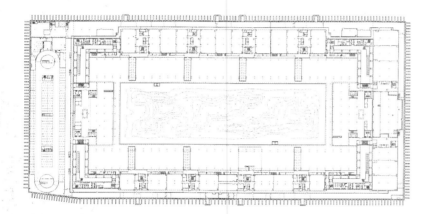

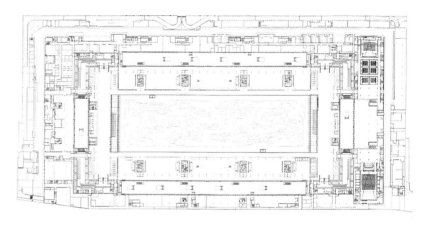

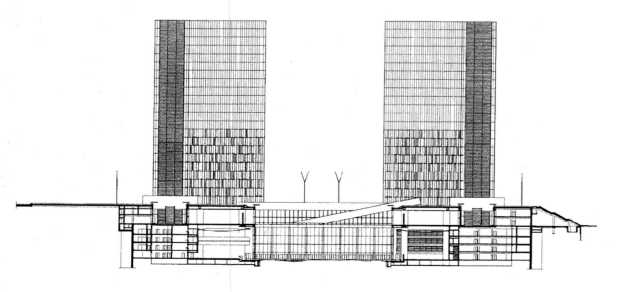

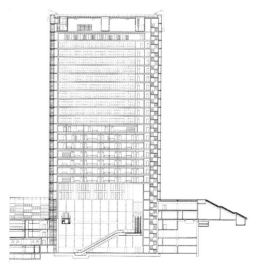

COUPE TRANSVERSALE SUR UNE TOUR
JANVIER 1995 · ech.1/500
BIBLIOTHÈQUE NATIONALE DE FRANCE
DOMINIQUE PERRAULT ARCHITECTE

France

France

Award Der große BDA-Preis (Gold Medal)
Given by Bund Deutscher Architekten (BDA)
Prize Presentation 1993
Members of the Jury Erhard Tränkner (BDA president), Uwe Köhnholdt,
Christoph Mäckler, Werner Strodthoff
Architect Thomas Herzog, Munich
Award Winning Building **All projects; here: Design Center, Linz**
Location Linz, Austria
Design and Construction Period 1989 - 1994

Design Team T. Herzog with H. J. Schrade; R. Schneider, A. Schankula,
K. Beslmüller, A. Heigl, O. Mehl; H. Stögmüller
Structural and Civil Engineering Fritz Sailer + Kurt Stepan, Munich
Environmental Engineering Constructional physics: Nils V. Waubke;
Daylight technology: Lichtplanung Christian Bartenbach; Energy simulation:
Fraunhofer-Institut für solare Energiesysteme, ISE
Mechanical and Electrical Engineering Mathias Bloos, Munich, with
Ökoenergie Greif, Wels
Interior Design Verena Herzog-Loibl, Munich
Approximate Cost ÖS 855,000,000
Site Area 34,200 m²
Building Area 16,800 m²
Total Floor Area 31,000 m²
Photography Dieter Leistner, Peter Bonfig

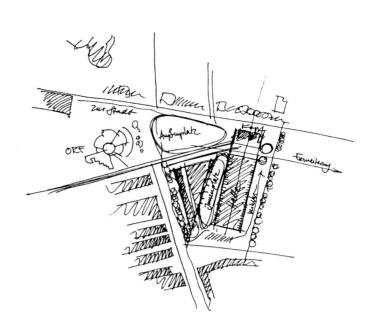

112 **Germany**
Thomas Herzog

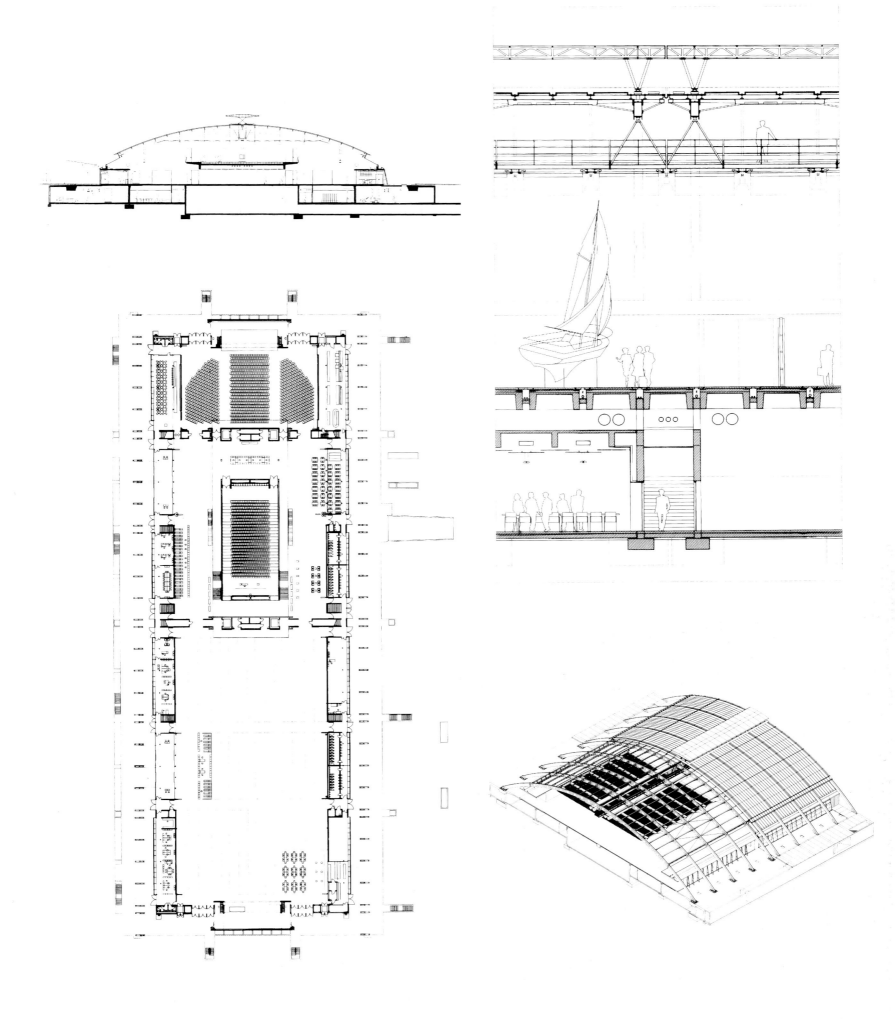

115

Germany

Award Certificate of Merit 1994
Given by The Hong Kong Institute of Architects
Prize Presentation March / 17 / 1995
Members of the Jury Victor So, Helen Yu, Kenneth Kan, Dominic Kwan,
Helena To, Tunney Lee
Architects Wong Tung & Partners Limited, Hong Kong
Award Winning Building **Dragon Centre**
Location 37K, Yen Chow Street, Sham Shui Po, Hong Kong
Design and Construction Period 1990 - 1994

Design Team Wong Tung & Partners Ltd.: William Wong Jr. (Principal),
Jim K. P. Tong (Director in charge of design), Owen K. W. Tang (Director in
charge of administration and production), K. S. Kwok, S. K. Say, Tony W. M.
Tang & Caroline K. Y. Ma (Project team)
Structural and Civil Engineering Ove Arup & Partners Hong Kong Ltd.
Quantity Surveying Levett & Bailey
Mechanical and Electrical Engineering J. Roger Preston & Partners
Interior Design Walker Group / CNI
Approximate Cost HK$ 800,000,000
Site Area 7,198 m²
Building Area 88,000 m²
Total Floor Area 77,738 m²

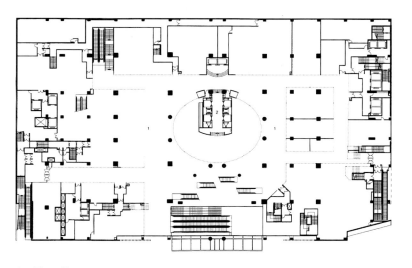

1st Floor Plan

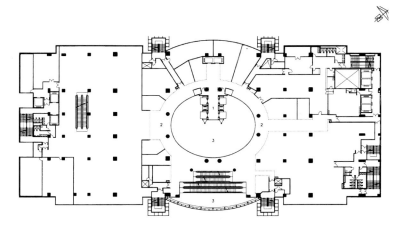

6th Floor Plan

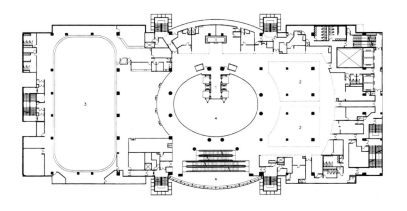

8th Floor Plan

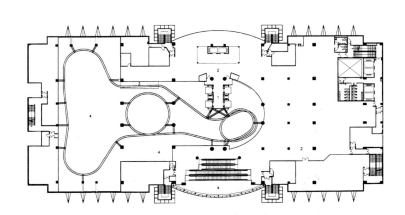

9th Floor Plan

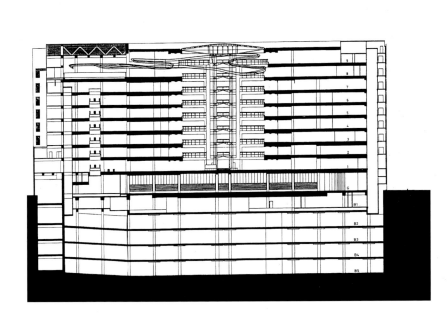

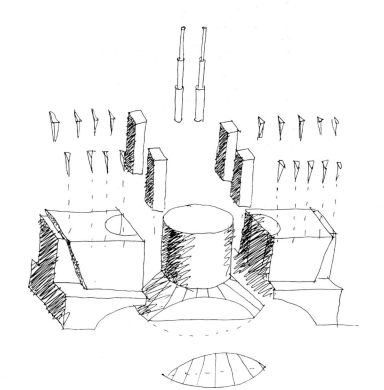

Hong Kong

Award Ybl Miklós Prize
Given by Ministry of Environmental Planning
Prize Presentation March / 15 / 1994
Architect Dezső Ekler
Award Winning Building **All projects; here: Cultural Camp in Nagykálló**
Location Nagykálló, Harangod, Hungary
Design and Construction Period 1986 - 1991

Structural and Civil Engineering Dezső Ekler
Environmental Engineering Dezső Ekler
Mechanical and Electrical Engineering Géza Matúz, Lajos Balogh
Interior Design Dezső Ekler
Landscape Architecture Dezső Ekler
Approximate Cost HUF 18,000,000
Site Area 220,000 m²
Building Area 690 m²
Total Floor Area 750 m²
Photography Miklós Csák, Róbert Szabó

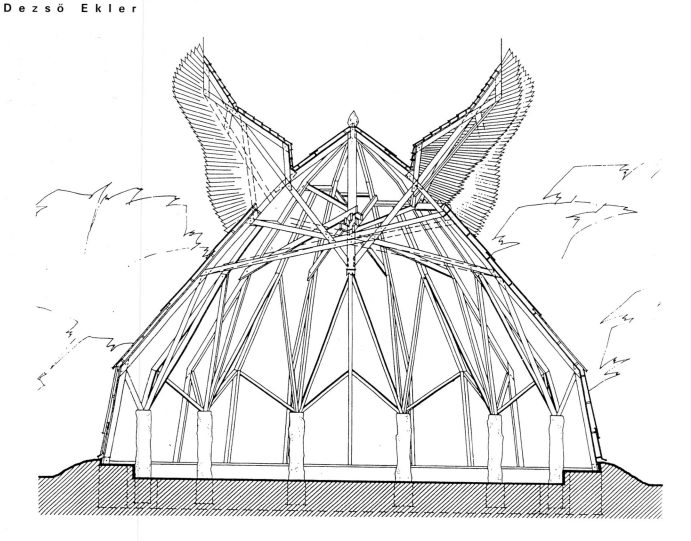

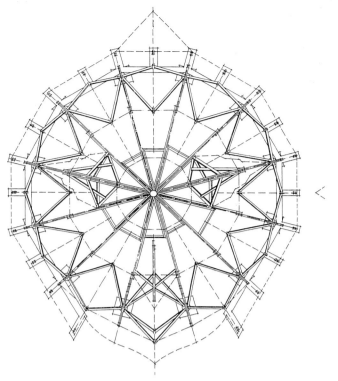

Cultural Camp, Dancing Barn

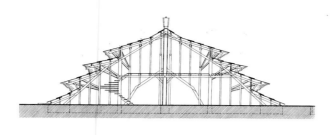
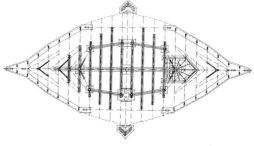

Cultural Camp, Reception Building

Cultural Camp, Eating Hall

123

Cultural Camp, Look-out Tower

Award 1- Award for Architectural Excellence / 2- RIAI / Regional Award
(Western)
Given by 1- The Architectural Association of Ireland / 2- The Royal
Institute of the Architects of Ireland
Prize Presentation 1- 1994; 2- 1993
Members of the Jury 1- John Hejduk, Shane de Blacam, Joan O`Connor,
Tom de Paor, Vivienne Roche; 2- Joan O'Connor, Denis Handy
Architects The Office of Public Works Architects, Dublin
Award Winning Building **The Céide Fields Visitor Centre**
Location Ballycastle, Co. Mayo, Ireland
Design and Construction Period 1990 - 1993

Design Team Mary MacKenna, Michael O'Doherty, Michael Haugh, Tony
O'Shaughnessy, Andrew Cooke, Sean Golden; Student assistants: L. Boyce,
N. Brown, I. Coveney, K. Kelliher, C. Payne, W. Rothwell, S. Thornton
Structural and Civil Engineering Concannon, Healy Heffernan
Quantity Surveying Fergal Coghlan Associates
Mechanical and Electrical Engineering Project Management Ltd.
Landscape Architecture Mitchell Associates
Approximate Cost £ 2,000,000
Site Area 1.5 ha
Building Area 750 m²
Total Floor Area 950 m²
Photography Con Brogan of O.P.W., John Searle

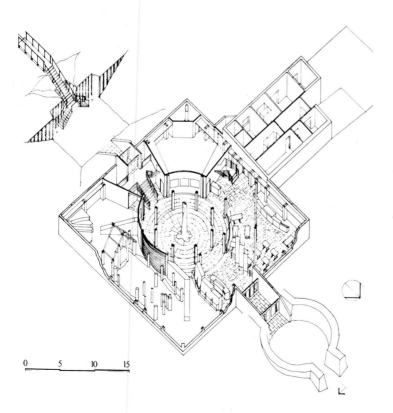

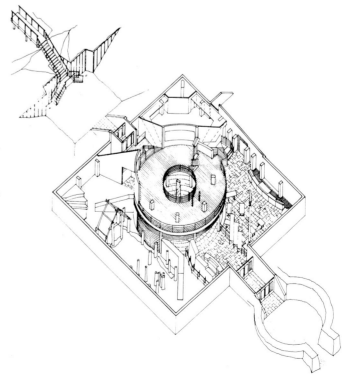

Award RIAI Regional Award (Southern)
Given by The Royal Institute of the Architects of Ireland, RIAI
Prize Presentation 1994
Architects The Office of Public Works Architects, Dublin
Award Winning Building **The Blasket Island Cultural Centre**
Location Kerry, Ireland
Design and Construction Period 1989 - 1993

Design Team The Office of Public Works Architects, Ciaran O'Connor
and Gerard O'Sullivan
Structural and Civil Engineering Walsh
Quantity Surveying Casey
Mechanical and Electrical Engineering Tuomey
Landscape Architecture The Office of Public Works Architects
Building Area 1,779 m^2

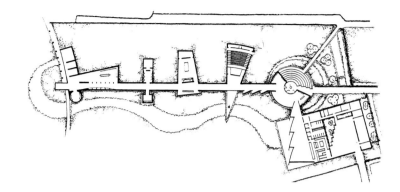

Award The JIA Prize for the Best Young Architect of the Year
Given by The Japan Institute of Architects (JIA)
Prize Presentation October /13 /1994
Members of the Jury Kitoh Azusa and others
Architect Hiroshi Miyazaki, Tokyo
Award Winning Building **Chuya Nakahara Memorial Museum**
Location Yamaguchi, Yamaguchi Prefecture, Japan
Design and Construction Period October 1992 - October 1993

Design Team Hiroshi Miyazaki (Plants Associates)
Structural and Civil Engineering T & A Associates
Quantity Surveying Futaba Quantity Surveying
Mechanical and Electrical Engineering Sogo Consultants
Interior Design Kei Miyazaki (Plants Associates) / Graphics
Approximate Cost 300,000,000 Yen
Site Area 1,114 m²
Building Area 369 m²
Total Floor Area 499 m²
Photography Toshiharu Kitajima

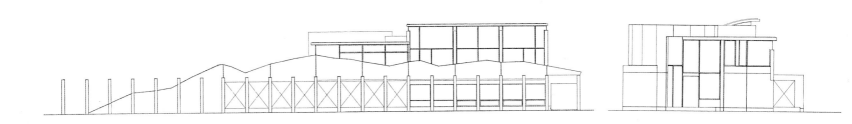

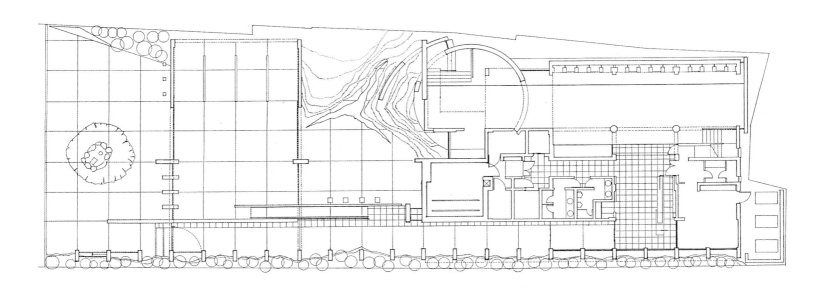

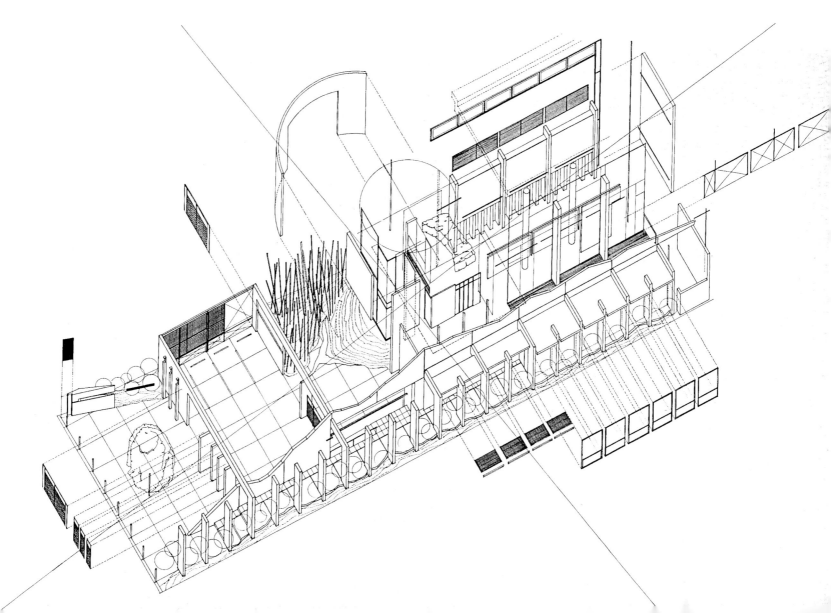

Japan

Award JIA Award for the Best Young Architect of the Year
Given by The Japan Institute of Architects, JIA
Prize Presentation September 1994
Architect Tadasu Ohe, Tokyo
Award Winning Building **Fun House**
Location 2 Ebisu Minami, Shibuya Ward, Tokyo, Japan
Design and Construction Period July 1991 - September 1993

Structural Engineering Alpha Structural Design
Mechanical and Electrical Engineering Fujigou Engineers Office, Inc.
and Marsumoto Electrical Designers (Facilities design)
Site Area 1,037.21 m²
Building Area 715.31 m²
Total Floor Area 3,206.32 m²
Photography Shinkenchiku-Sha

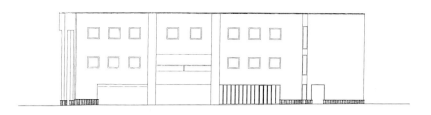

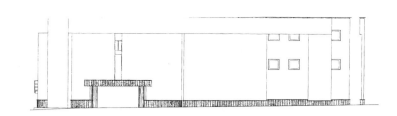

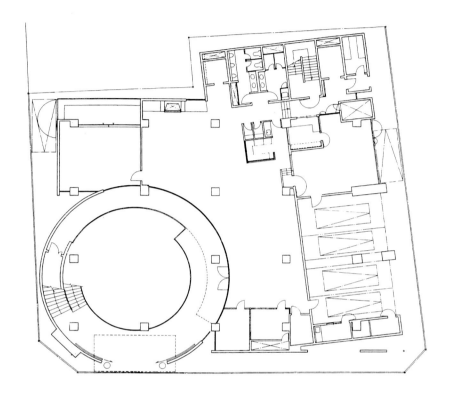

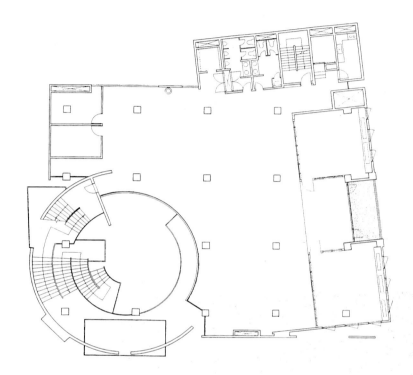

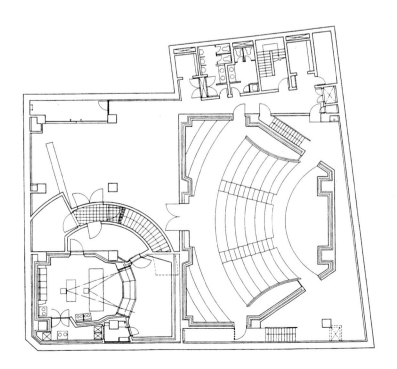

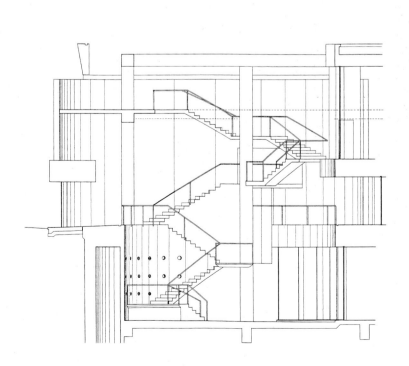

Award Le Prix de l'Union des Architectes de la République du Kazakhstan
Given by L'Union des Architectes du Kazakhstan
Prize Presentation 1995
Prize Winner Alberto Campo Baeza, Madrid
Award Winning Building **Looking at the sea, Public School**
Location Cadiz, Spain
Design and Construction Period 1989 - 1991

Approximate Cost US$ 2,800,000
Site Area 2,016 m²
Building Area 4,320 m²

138   **Kazakhstan**
Alberto Campo Baeza

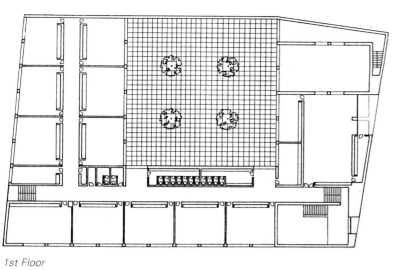

1st Floor

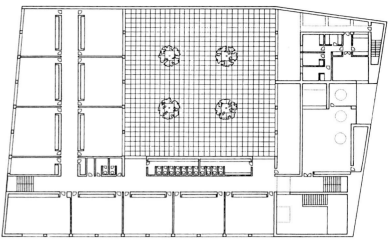

2nd Floor

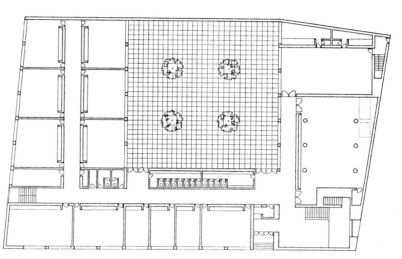

Ground Floor

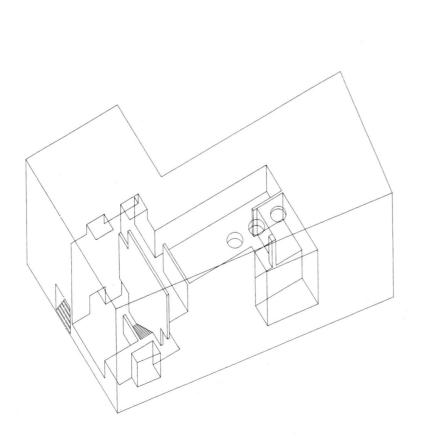

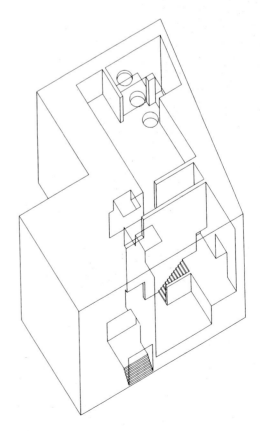

Kazakhstan

Award Prix Luxembourgeois d'Architecture

Given by Ordre des Architectes et des Ingénieurs Conseils Fondation de l'Architecture et de l'Ingénieurie

Prize Presentation November / 10 / 1995

Members of the Jury S. Beel, J. Flammang, E. Lunghi, B. Paczowski, D. Perrault

Architects Hermann & Valentiny, Architectes, Vienna / Luxembourg

Award Winning Building **Luxembourg Embassy, Vienna**

Location Sternwartestrasse 81, Vienna, Austria

Design and Construction Period 1992 -1994

Structural and Civil Engineering H. Endl

Mechanical and Electrical Engineering Hermann & Valentiny

Interior Design Hermann & Valentiny

Landscape Architecture Hermann & Valentiny

Approximate Cost ÖS 12,000,000

Site Area 915 m²

Building Area 162.54 m²

Total Floor Area 497.62 m²

Photography Margherita Spiluttini, Vienna

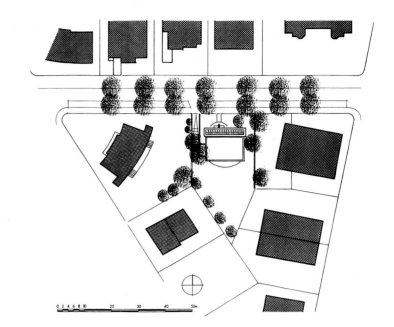

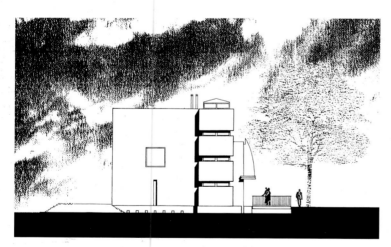

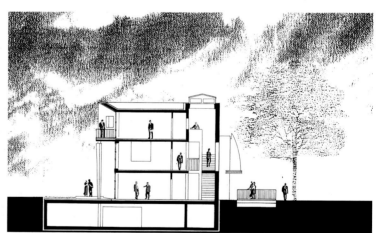

Luxembourg

Award / Recommendation of Chamber of Architects and Civil Engineers
of Malta
Given by Chamber of Architects and Civil Engineers of Malta
Prize Winner Architecture Project
Award Winning Building **Corporate Offices for L. Farrugio & Sons Ltd.**
Location Hamrun, Malta
Design and Construction Period 1991 -1994

Design Team Alberto Miceli Farrugio (project leader), David Felice, Joanna
Spiteri-Staines, Louis Attard, Marisa O'Clock, Sandie Galea
Structural and Civil Engineering Dion Buhagiar (Company: TBR Structural
Engineers), Pierre Zammit
Interior Design Architecture Project with Marisa O'Clock
Landscape Architecture Architecture Project with Peter Calamatta
Approximate Cost US $ 370,000,000
Site Area 8.200 m²
Building Area 800 m²
Total Floor Area 1.000 m²
Photography David Pisani (Company: Working Lights Ltd.)

Award National Steel Award

Given by Stichting Nederlandse Staalbouw

Prize Presentation October 1994

Members of the Jury Jan Brouwer and others

Architect Maarten Struijs, Rotterdam

Award Winning Building **Smoke Cleaner AVI Brielselaan**

Location Rotterdam, The Netherlands

Design and Construction Period 1991 - 1993

Design Team Public Works Rotterdam

Structural and Civil Engineering Public Works Rotterdam

Mechanical and Electrical Engineering Tebodin, The Hague

Approximate Cost Hfl 365,000,000

Photography Michel Hofmeester, Piet Rook

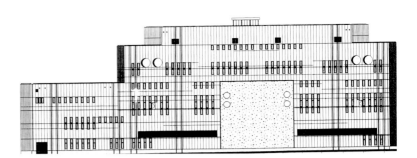

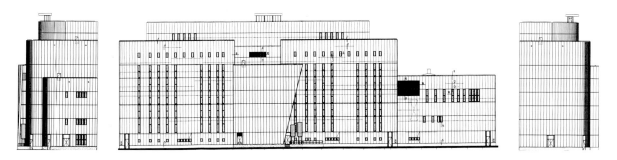

Award BNA Kubus

Given by Bond van Nederlandse Architecten (BNA)

Prize Presentation July / 1 / 1994

Architects Aldo and Hannie van Eyck, Amsterdam

Award Winning Building **Church for the Moluccan Community of Deventer**

Location Deventer, The Netherlands

Design and Construction Period 1984 - 1992

Structural and Civil Engineering Heijckmann B.V.

Quantity Surveying Aldo and Hannie van Eyck

Mechanical and Electrical Engineering Van Dijk B.V.

Interior Design Aldo and Hannie van Eyck

Landscape Architecture Aldo and Hannie van Eyck

Approximate Cost Hfl 1,200,000

Site Area approx. 2,600 m²

Building Area approx. 550 m²

Total Floor Area +/- 17 x 32 m² - interior height +/- 3 m

Photography Herman van Doom

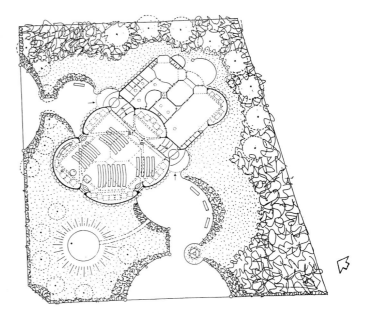

The Netherlands

Aldo and Hannie van Eyck

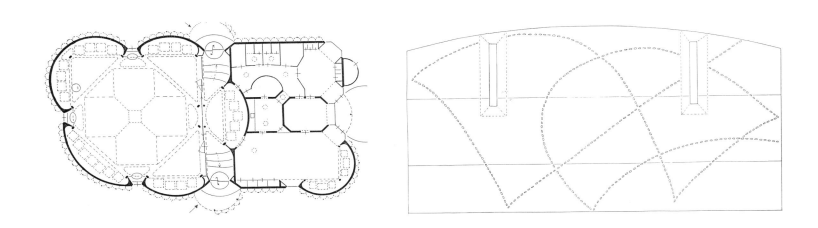

151

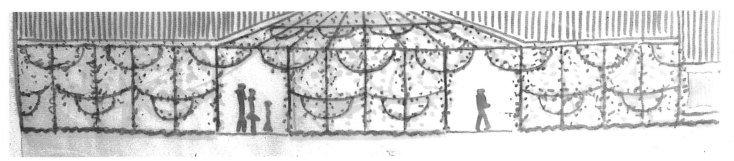

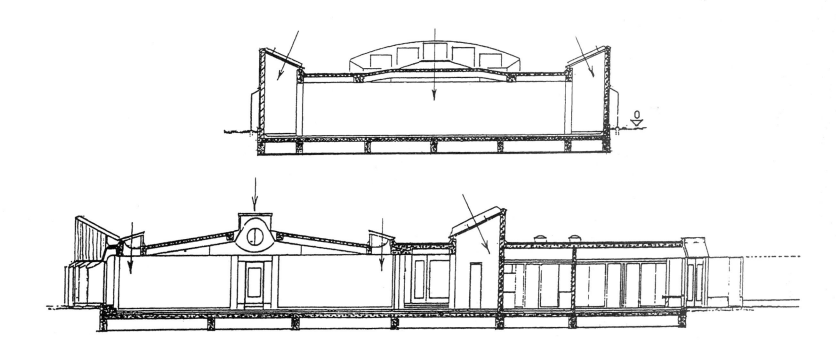

The Netherlands

Award A. J. van Eyck Prize

Given by A. J. van Eyck Stichting

Prize Presentation September 1990

Members of the Jury W. G. Qu st, J. Benthem, A. Bodon, L. J. Heijdenrijk, J. Oosterhof

Architect Koen van Velsen, Bussum

Award Winning Building **Public Library Zeewolde**

Location Zeewolde, The Netherlands

Design and Construction Period 1986 - 1989

Structural and Civil Engineering Bouwadviesburo Strackee Amsterdam

Mechanical and Electrical Engineering Technisch adviesburo Treffers & Partners

Interior Design Koen van Velsen

Approximate Cost Hfl 1,624,000

Site Area 840 m²

Building Area 555 m²

Total Floor Area +/ - 1,250 m²

Photography Gerhard Jaeger

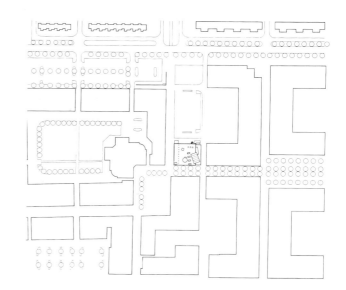

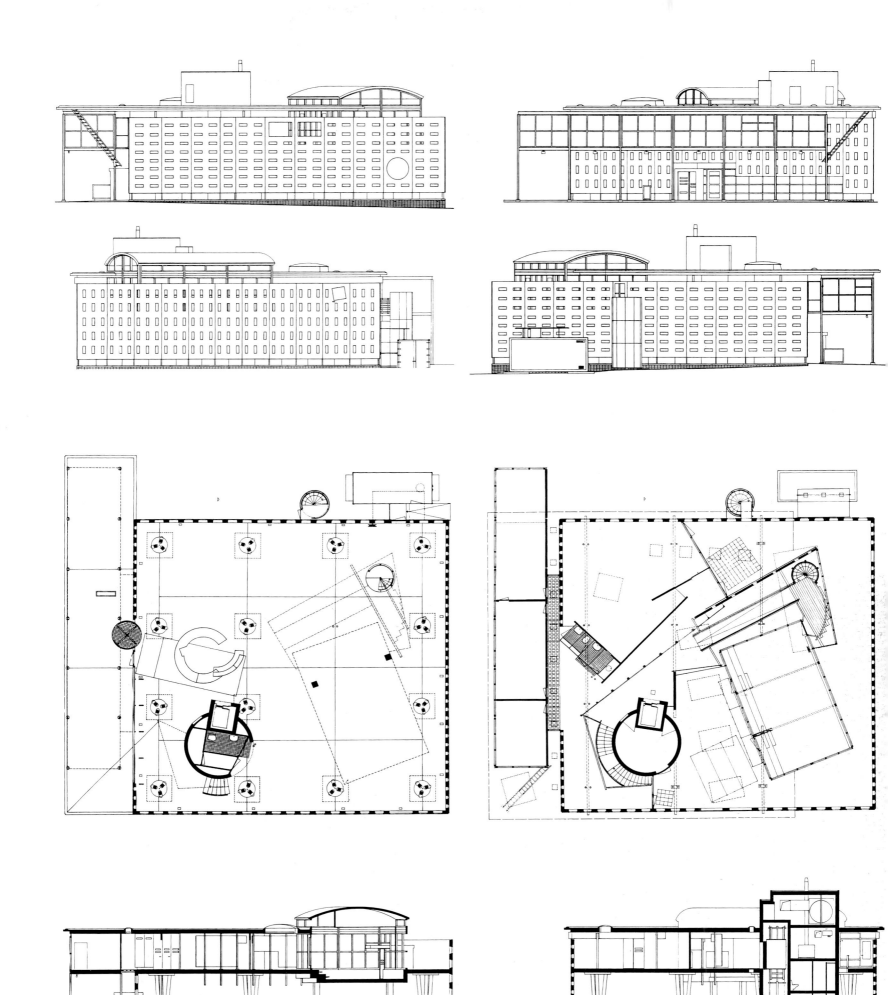

The Netherlands

Award Anton Christian Houens Fonds Diplom

Given by The Department of Culture, presented by the Minister of Culture
Åse Klevland

Prize Presentation October 1994

Members of the Jury Morton Løvseth, Eilif Bjørge, Trine Sylten, Ragna
Weider, Ulf Grønvold

Architects Arkitektkontoret Kari Nissen Brodtkorb, Eiksmarka

Award Winning Building **›Stranden‹**

Location Aker Brygge, Oslo, Norway

Design and Construction Period 1988 -1991

Design Team Arkitektkontoret Kari Nissen Brodtkorb as. with Kari Nissen
Brodtkorb, Randi Fredriksen, Maj Jøsok

Structural and Civil Engineering Arne Hill as.

Quantity Surveying Arkitektkontoret Kari Nissen Brodtkorb as.

Mechanical and Electrical Engineering Berg-Nilsen & Reinertsen as.

Interior Design Arkitektkontoret Kari Nissen Brodtkorb as.

Landscape Architecture Arkitektkontoret Kari Nissen Brodtkorb as. and
13.3 Landskapsarkitekter as.

Building Area 3,500 m²

Total Floor Area 26,500 m²

Photography Jim Bengston, Randi Fredriksen, Kari Nissen Brodtkorb

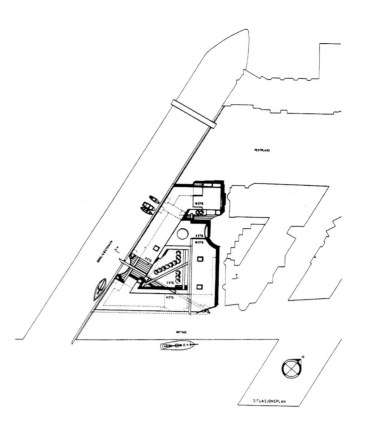

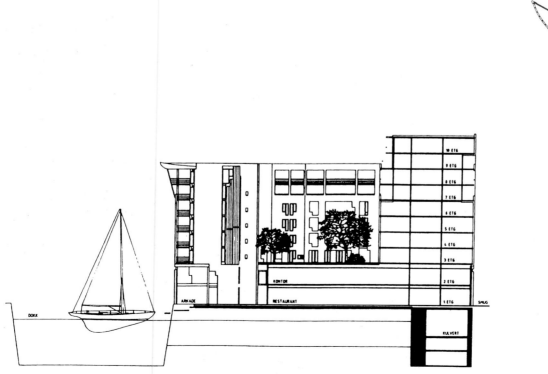

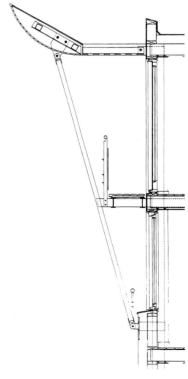

Norway

Norway

Award Houens Fond
Given by Ministry of Culture
Prize Presentation 1994
Members of the Jury Morten Løvseth, Eilif Bjorge, Trine Sylten,
Ragna Weiden
Architect Sverre Fehn, Oslo
Award Winning Building **Glasier Museum**
Location Fjærland, Norway
Design and Construction Period 1989 -1991

Design Team Sverre Fehn - Henrik Hille Architects M. N. A. L.
Structural and Civil Engineering SIV. Engineer Terje Orlien
Quantity Surveying SIV. Engineer Wilhelm Andenæs
Approximate Cost NOK 15,000,000
Building Area 1,250 m²
Photography Terje Solvang, Guy Fehn, Per Olaf Fjeld

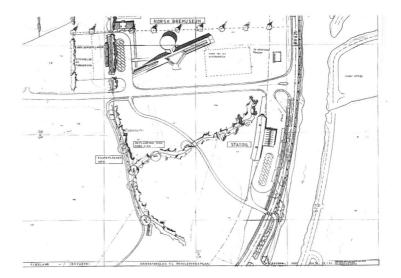

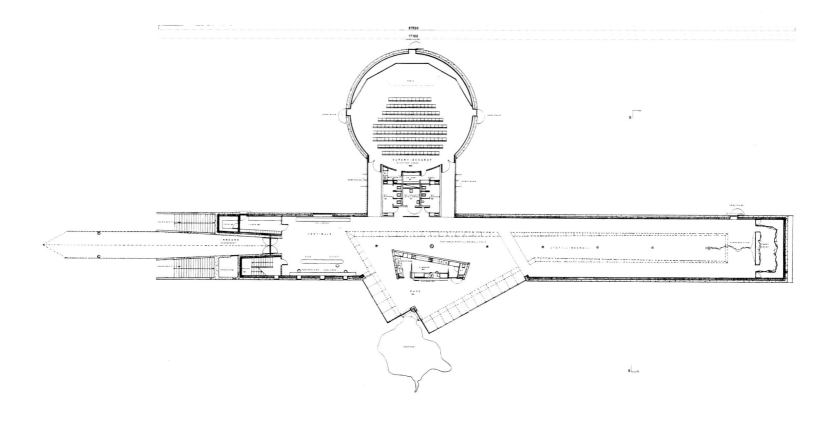

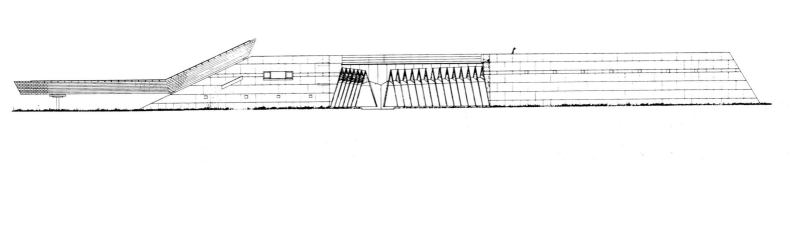

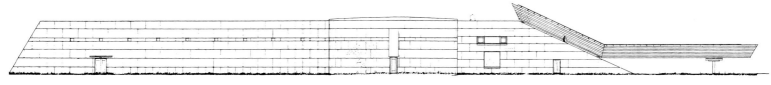

Norway

Norway

Award Hexagono de Oro, VIII Bienal de Arquitectura
Given by Colegio de Arquitectos del Perú
Architects Oscar Borasino, Jose Antonio Vallarino, Miraflores
Award Winning Building **Chapel of the Reconciliation**
(Capilla de la Reconciliacion)
Design and Construction Period 1990 - 1992

Structural and Civil Engineering Alberto Merino
Sanitary and Electrical Project Diaz + Deustua
Building Area 1,750 m²

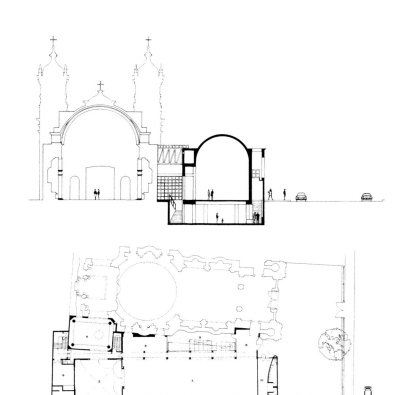

166   Peru
Osacar Borasino, Jose Antonio Vallarino

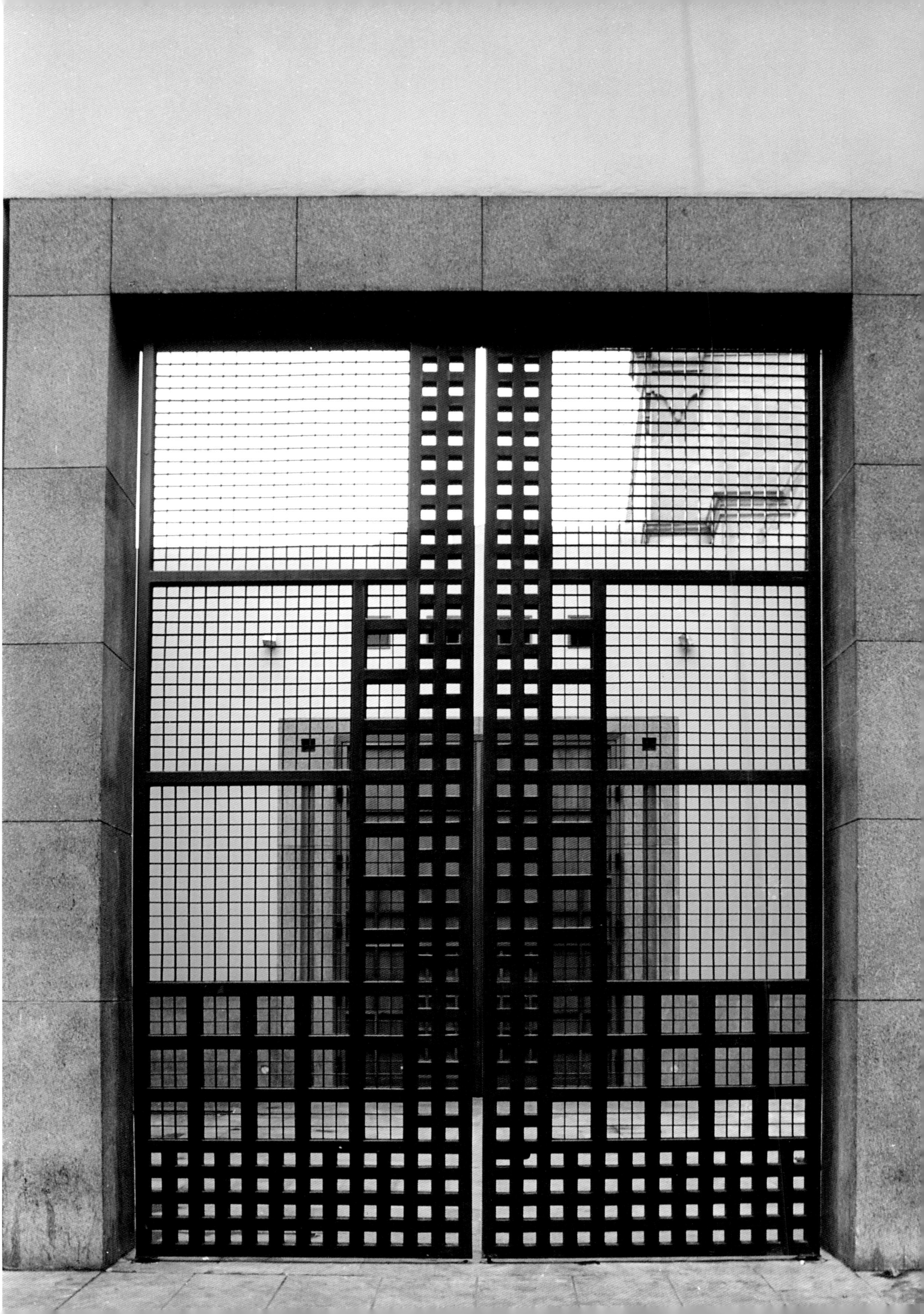

169

Award 1- Premio Ciutat de Barcelona 1. Premio / 2- Premio Fad de
Arquitectura 1. Premio
Given by 1- Ayuntamiento de Barcelona / 2- Asociacion Fad de Barcelona
Prize Presentation 1-1994; 2-1994
Architects Viaplana / Piñon Arqs. R. Mercadé ASS., Barcelona
Award Winning Building **Centro de Cultura Contemporanea,**
Casa de Caritat
Location Calle Montalegre 5, Barcelona, Spain
Design and Construction Period 1990 - 1993

Design Team Albert Viaplana I Vea (project); Viaplana / Piñon Arqs.
R. Mercadé ASS. in collaboration with David Viaplana, Aurora Fernandez
Structural and Civil Engineering Brufau / Obiol / Moya
Approximate Cost Pts 3,500 million
Building Area 4,500 m² (new); 10,400 m² (conversion)
Photography Ferran Freixa

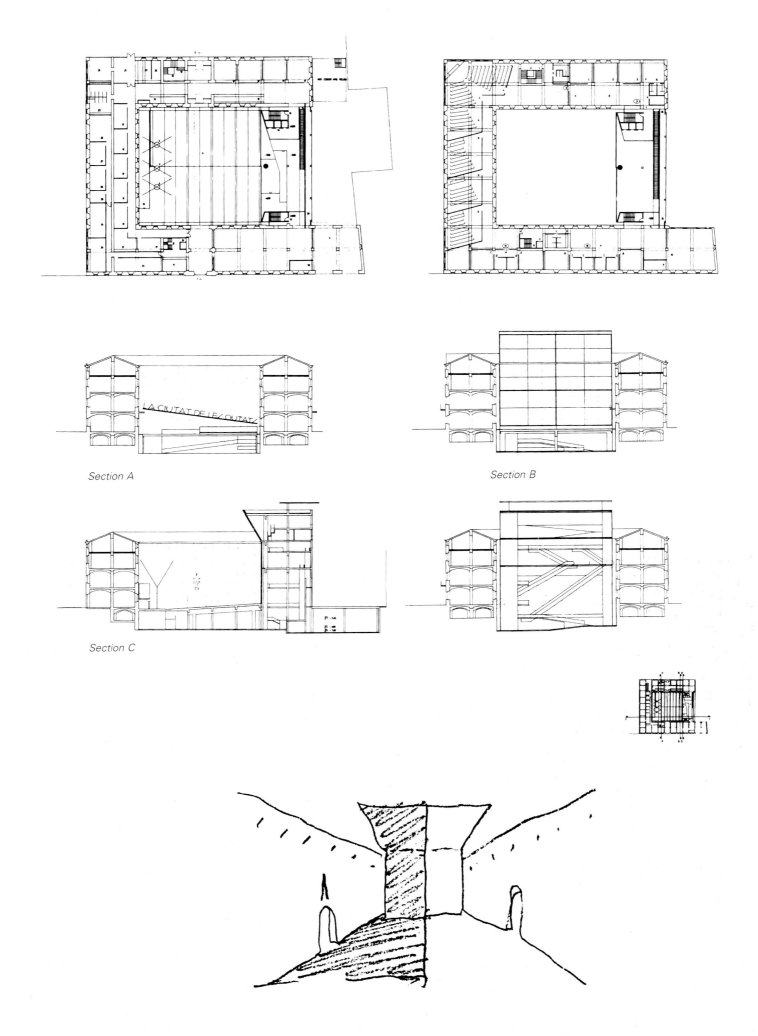

Section A

Section B

Section C

172

Spain

Spain

Award SARs Kasper Salin-Pris
Given by Svenska Arkitekters Ri<sförbund (SAR) - The National Association
of Swedish Architects
Prize Presentation 1994
Members of the Jury Jens Arnfred, Krister Bjurström, Stefan Alenius,
Mats Edblom
Architects Rosenbergs Arkitekter AB together with Tekniska Verken i
Linköping AB, Stockholm
Award Winning Building **Tekniska Verken i Linköping AB**
Location Linköping, Sweden
Design and Construction Period 1988 - 1993

Design Team Rosenbergs Arkitekter AB, Stockholm
Structural and Civil Engineering Jacobson & Widmark, Linköping
Mechanical and Electrical Engineering Theorells Ingenjörsbyrå and
Elpa Mitt, Linköping
Interior Design Rosenbergs Arkitekter AB (partly)
Landscape Architecture Gunnar Martinsson Landskapsarkitekter AB
Approximate Cost Skr 290,000,000
Site Area approx. 45,000 m²
Building Area approx. 30,000 m² (netarea)
Total Floor Area 34,600 m² (grossarea; garages and parking included)
Photography Åke Eison Linnman

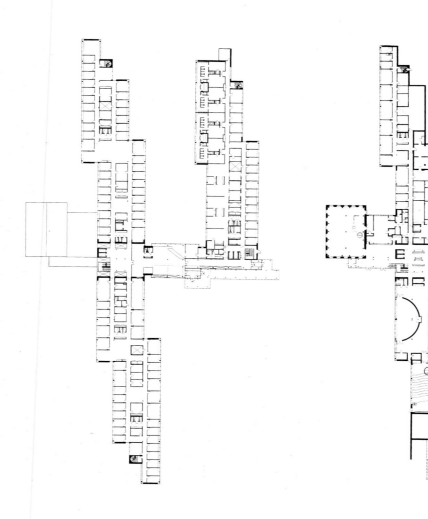

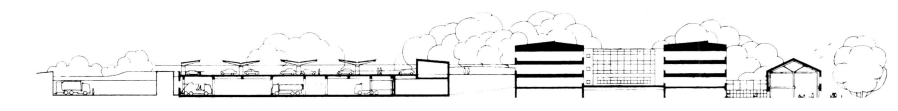

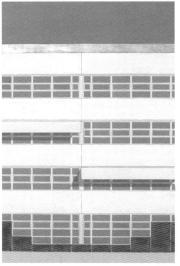

Sweden

Award Prix Interassar

Given by Intergroupe des Associations d'Architectes

Prize Presentation January 1995

Members of the Jury S. Vuarraz, P. Heiniger, B. Crettaz, F. Goetschmann, H. Presset, Ph. Renaud, A. Spitsas

Architects Peter Böcklin, Predrag Petrovic, Geneva

Award Winning Building **Théâtre de l'Enfance et de la Jeunesse**
A. Chavanne

Location 56, Route de Frontenex, Geneva, Switzerland

Construction Period 1988 - 1992

Design Team Atelier d'Architecture P. Böcklin (P. Böcklin, R. Fabra, N. Maeder, B. Porcher)

Structural and Civil Engineering C. Fischer SA

Mechanical and Electrical Engineering Paschoud Engineering

Interior Design Atelier d'Architecture P. Böcklin

Landscape Architecture Atelier d'Architecture P. Böcklin

Approximate Cost SFr 16,460,000

Site Area 1,326 m²

Building Area 903 m²

Total Floor Area 3,110 m²

Photography Roy Robel / Workshop

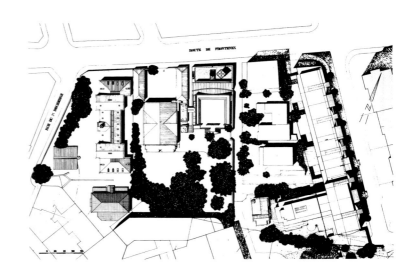

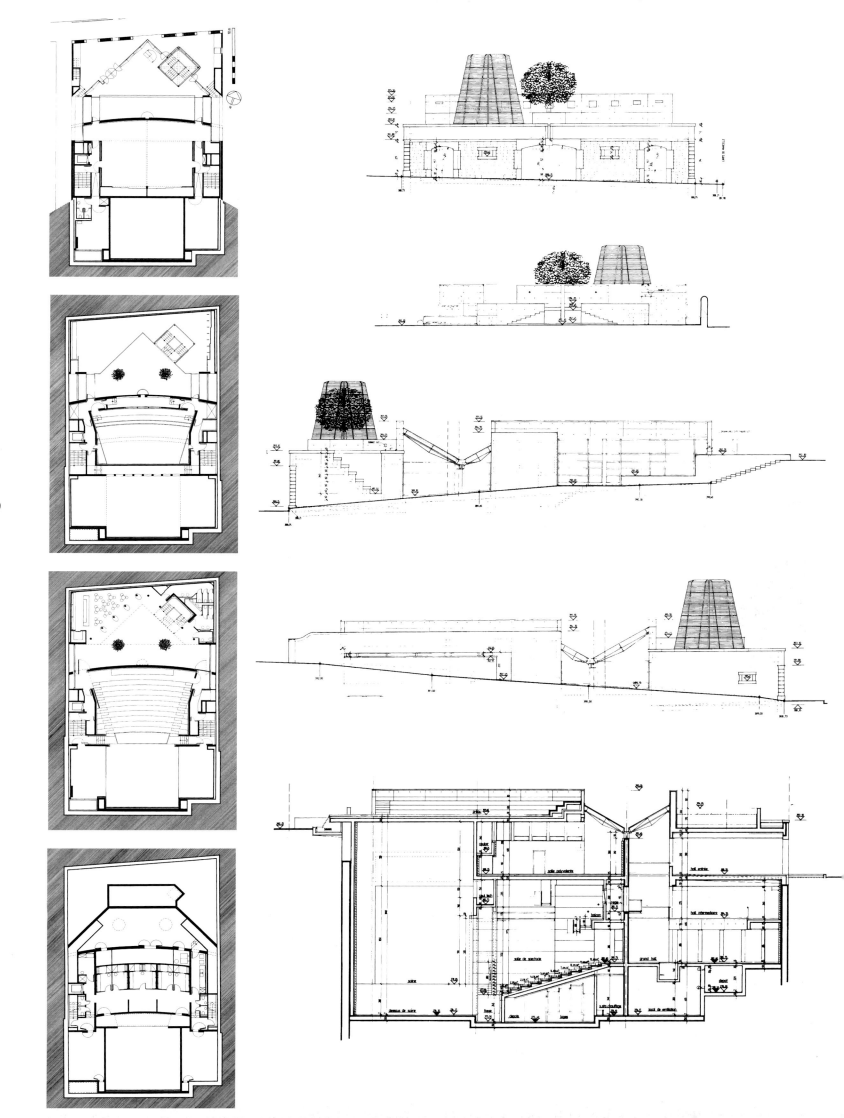

Switzerland

Award Auszeichnung für gute Bauten der Stadt Zürich
Given by Hochbauamt Zürich (on behalf of the Schweizerischer Ingenieur-
und Architektenverein)
Prize Presentation 1995
Members of the Jury Ursula Koch, Kathrin Martelli, Hans Rudolf Rüegg,
Hans Kollhoff, Karljosef Schattner, Peter Zumthor, Dieter Nievergelt,
Beat Maeschi, Dominik Bachmann
Architects Trix and Robert Haussmann and Steiger Partner, Architekten
und Planer AG, Hansruedi Stierli, Zurich
Award Winning Building **S-bahn station Museumsstrasse and
underground shopping malls**
Location Main Station, Zurich, Switzerland
Design and Construction Period completion of the station: 1990;
completion of the shops: 1991

Design Team Trix and Robert Haussmann and Hansruedi Stierli
Lighting Consultants Christian Bartenbach, Aldrans bei Innsbruck
(collaboration: Robert Gratzel, Robert Müller)

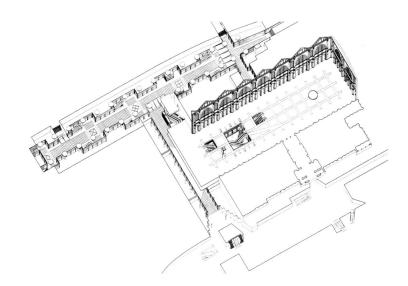

T r i x   a n d   R o b e r t   H a u s s m a n n   a n d   H a n s r u e d i   S t i e r l i

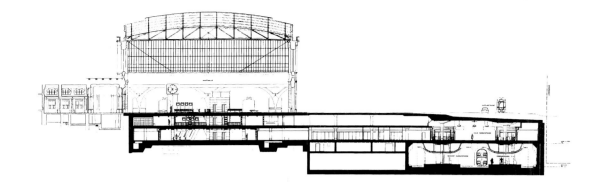

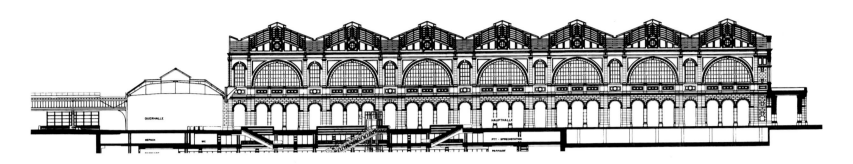

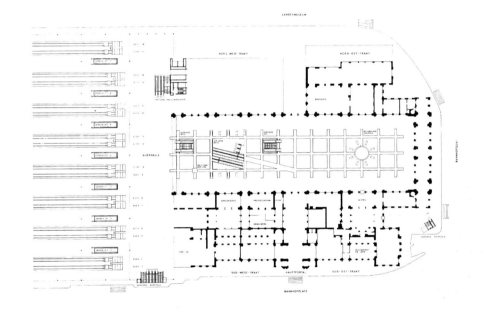

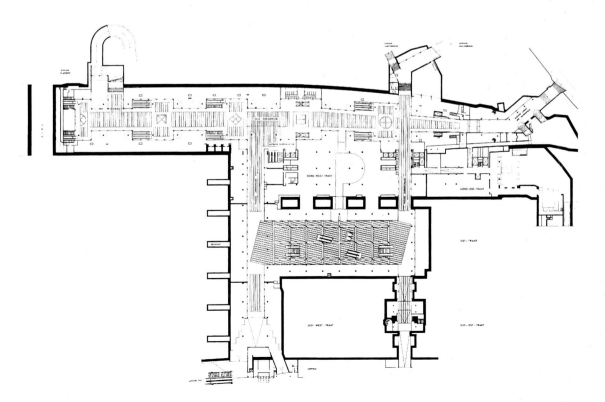

Switzerland

Award RIBA Regional Architecture Award (England, South West Region)
Given by Royal Institute of British Architects, RIBA
Prize Presentation 1994
Architects Nicholas Grimshaw & Partners Ltd., London
Award Winning Building **Western Morning News Headquarters & Print Works, Plymouth**
Location Plymouth, United Kingdom
Design and Construction Period 1990 - 1993

Design Team Nicholas Grimshaw & Partners: Nicholas Grimshaw,
Lindy Atkin, Eoin Billings, Paul Grayshon, Andrew Hall, Duncan Jackson,
Jonathan Leah, Nicola MacDonald, Christopher Nash, Julian Scanlan,
Matthew Seabrook, Mike Waddington, Martin Wood
Structural and Environmental Engineering Ove Arup & Partners
Quantity Surveying Davis Langdon & Everest
Acoustic Engineering Applied Acoustic Design
Mechanical and Electrical Engineering Cundall Jonston & Partners
Interior Design Nicholas Grimshaw & Partners
Landscape Architecture Edwards Gale
Approximate Cost £ 14,900,000
Cross-Floor Areas 5,671 m² (offices), 6,459 m² (production areas)
Photography Jo Reid and John Peck

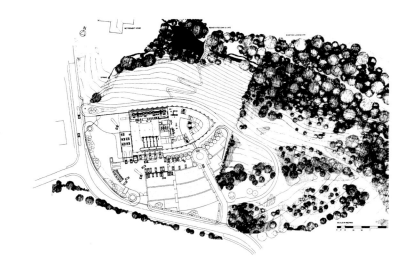

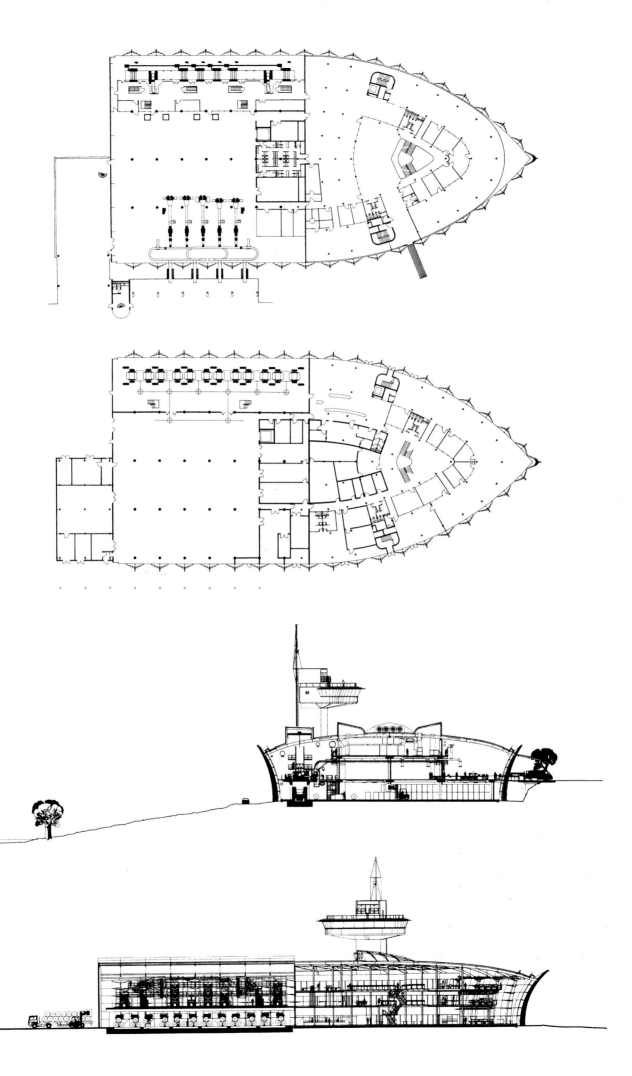

189

Award RIBA Regional Architecture Award (England, South East Region)
Given by Royal Institute of British Architects, RIBA
Prize Presentation 1994
Architects Michael Hopkins & Partners, London
Award Winning Building **Glyndebourne Opera House**
Location Lewes, East Sussex, United Kingdom
Design and Construction Period February 1989 - December 1993

Design Team Sir Michael Hopkins, Lady Hopkins, Robin Snell (Project
architect), Andrew Barnett, Pamela Bate, Arif Mehmood, Peter Cartwright,
Andrew Wells, Lucy Lavers, Edward Williams, Nigel Curry
Structural and Civil Engineering Ove Arup & Partners
Quantity Surveying Gardiner & Theobald
Mechanical and Electrical Engineering Ove Arup & Partners
Acoustic Consultants Arup Acoustics
Theatre Consultants Theatre Project Consultants
Approximate Cost £ 22,600,000
Total Floor Area 12,140 m²
Photography Martin Charles, Richard Davies

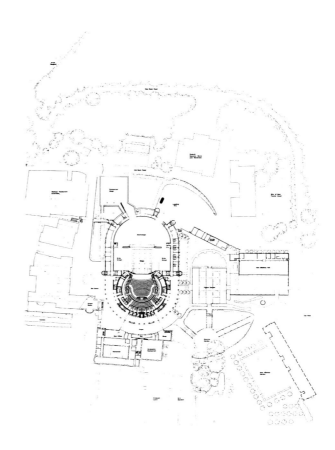

Michael Hopkins & Partners

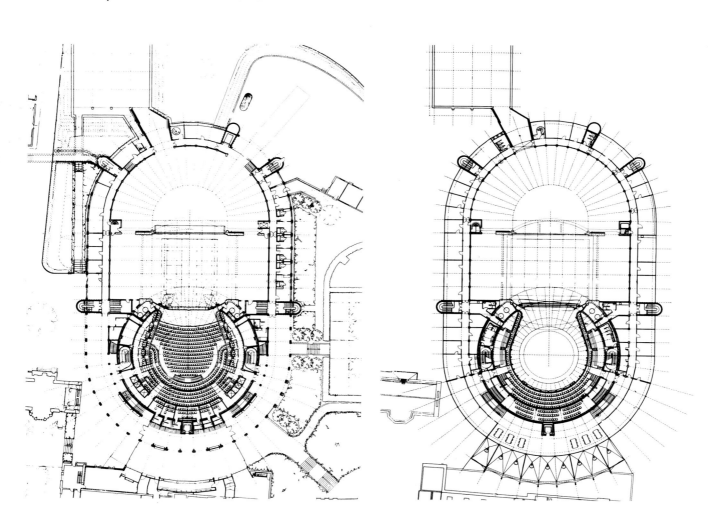

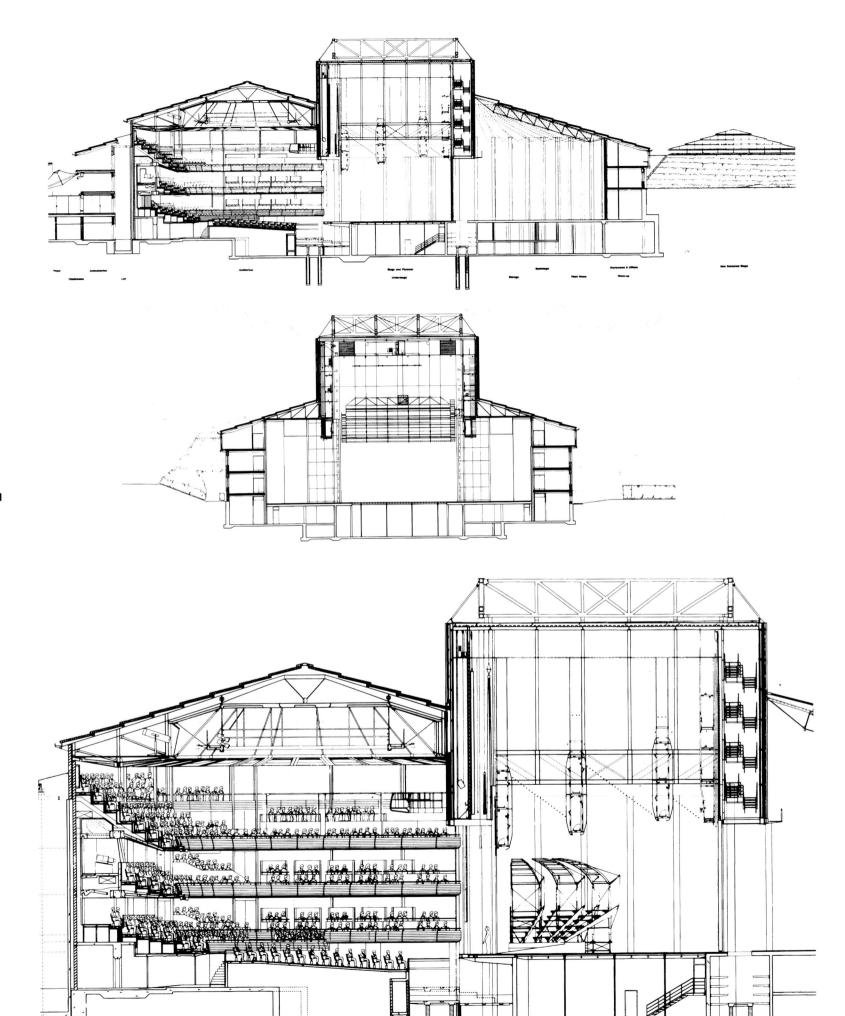

Award RIBA Regional Architecture Award (Wales)
Given by Royal Institute of British Architects, RIBA
Prize Presentation 1995
Architects Niall Phillips Architects Ltd, Bristol
Award Winning Building **The Welsh Wildlife Centre**
Location Teifi Marshes, Cilgerran, Nr. Cardigan, Dyfed, United Kingdom
Design and Construction Period 9 months

Structural and Civil Engineering Thorburn Colquhoun, Narberth
Quantity Surveying Wheeler Group Consultancy
Approximate Cost £ 600,000
Building Area 600 m²
Photography Charlotte Wood

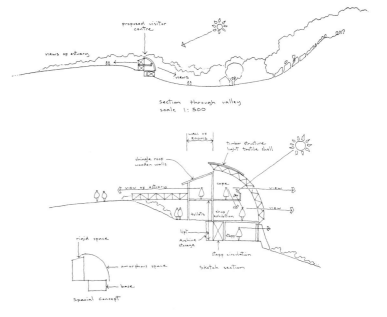

194 United Kingdom

Niall Phillipps Architects Ltd.

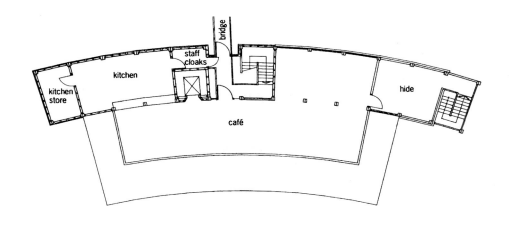

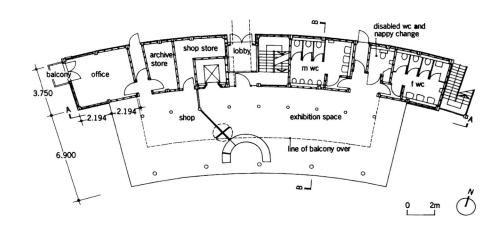

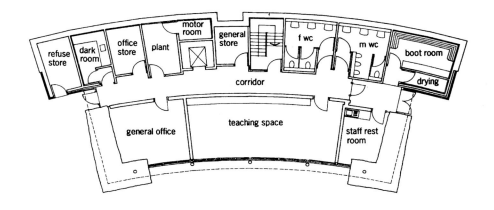

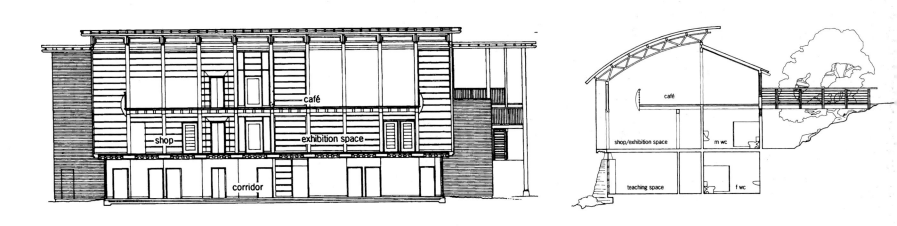

196

Award RIBA Regional Architecture Award (England, Southern Region)

Given by Royal Institute of British Architects, RIBA

Prize Presentation September 1994

Architects RHWL, Whitby & Bird (for bridge)

Award Winning Building **The Anvil, Basingstoke**

Location Churchill Way, Basingstoke, Hampshire, United Kingdom

Design and Construction Period July 1991 - April 1994

Architects and Theatre Planners / Designers RHWL, Nicholas Thompson,

Norman Bragg, Philip Christodoulou, Nicola Cowper, Ljiljana Blagojevic,

Susie Bridges, Dino Chandegara, Ashley Davies, Mike Fitzgerald,

Paul Smith, Alan Stanton

Structural and Services Engineering Whitby & Bird

Quantity Surveying Bucknall Austin

Mechanical and Electrical Engineering Mechanical: Crown House,

Electrical: Hall Electrical

Interior Design Clare Ferraby

Acousticians Arup Acoustics

Lighting Lighting Design Partnership

Approximate Cost £ 12,400,000

Site Area 0.42 ha

Building Area 2,600 m²

Total Floor Area 3,402 m²

Photography RHWL

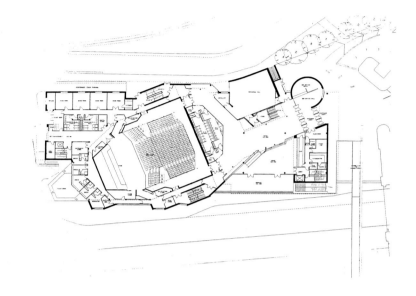

198 **United Kingdom**

RHWL, Whitby & Bird

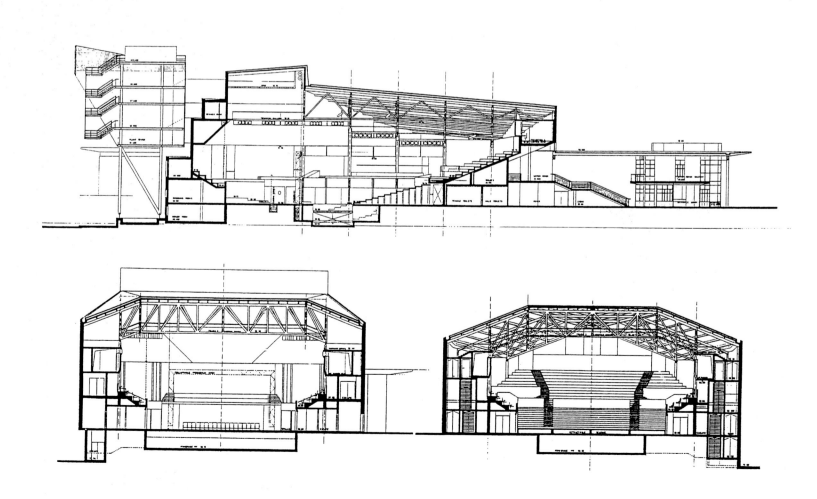

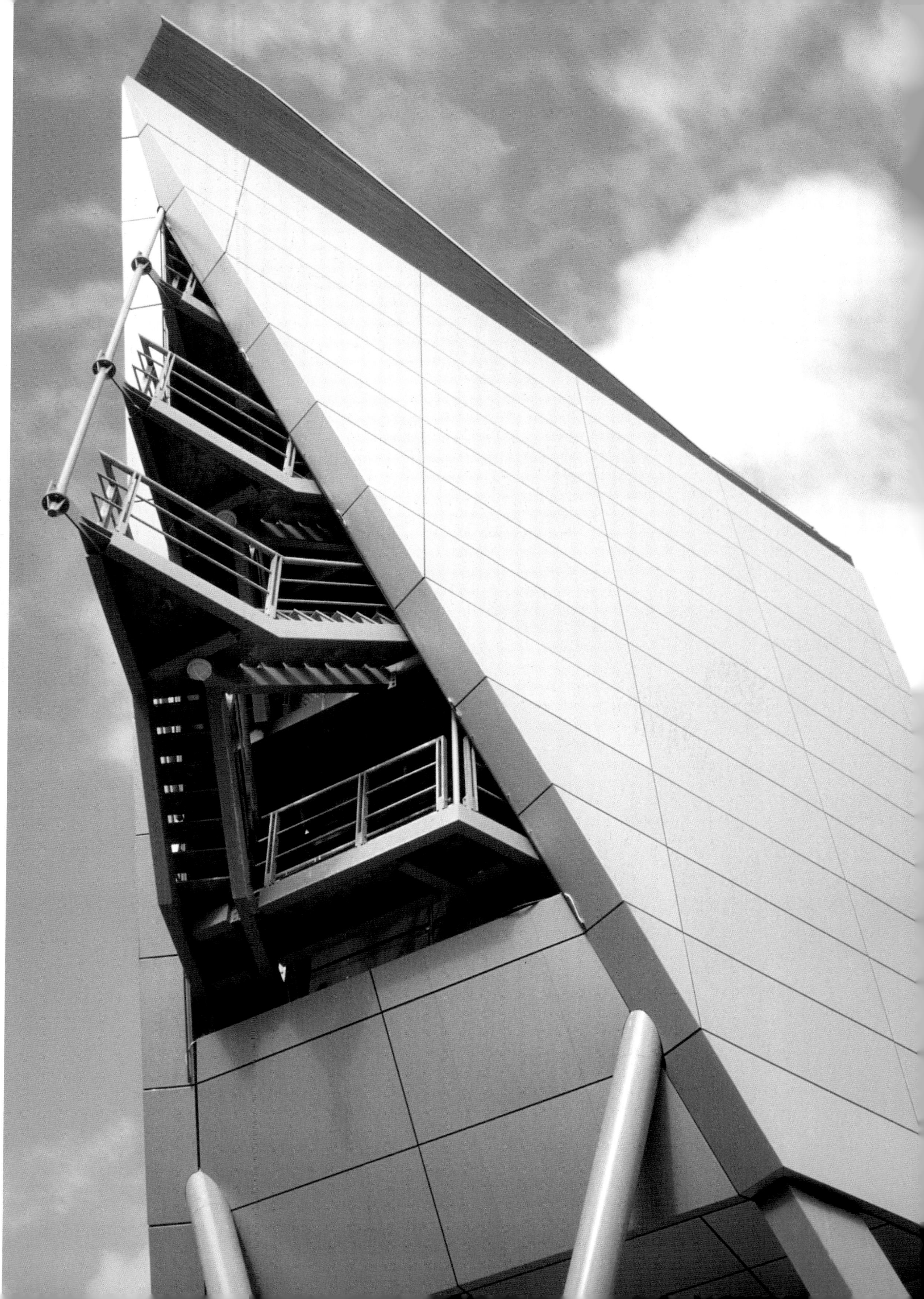

United Kingdom

Award 1- AIA National Honor Award for Architecture / 2- AIA Excellence
in Design Award / 3- AIA Design Award

Given by 1- The American Institute of Architects (AIA); 2- AIA, New York
State; 3- AIA New York City

Prize Presentation May 1994

Members of the Jury 1- Donlyn Lyndon, Ted Flato, Raymand Gindroz,
Jan Abell, Peter Van Dijk, Betsy West, Adele Chatfield-Taylor, Robert A.
Barthelman, Magali Sarfatti Larson

Architect Michael Fieldman & Partners, New York

Award Winning Building **Primary / Intermediate School 217**

Location Roosevelt Island (Manhattan), New York, USA

Design and Construction Period August 1989 - September 1992

Design Team Michael Fieldman, Miles Cigolle, Ed Rawlings, Clint Diener,
Charles Orton, David Hendershot

Quantity Surveying Federman Design and Construction

Interior Design Michael Fieldman & Partners

Landscape Architecture Michael Fieldman & Partners

Approximate Cost US$ 24,000,000

Site Area 55,000 sq. ft.

Building Area 105,000 sq. ft.

Total Floor Area 105,000 sq. ft.

Photography Chuck Choi

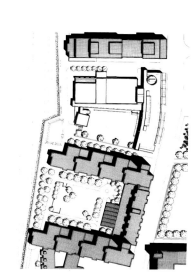

Michael Fieldman & Partners

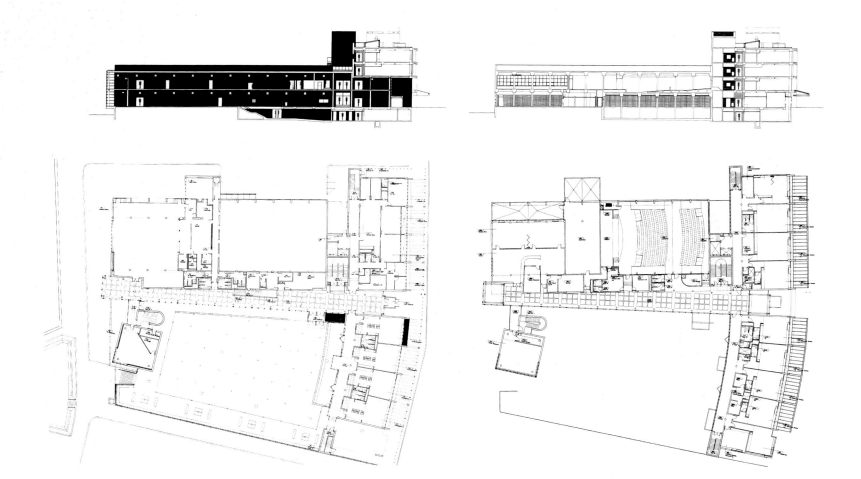

204

Award AIA Gold Medal

Given by The American Institute of Architects

Prize Presentation February 1994

Architect Sir Norman Foster, London/Berlin/Frankfurt/Glasgow/Hong Kong/Tokyo

Award Winning Building All projects; here: **Stansted Airport**

Location Stansted, London, United Kingdom

Design and Construction Period completed in 1991

Design Team Sir Norman Foster & Partners

Structural Engineering Ove Arup and Partners

Quantity Surveying BAAC with Beard Dove and Currie & Brown

Environmental Services, Drainage and Fire BAAC

Construction Management Laing Management Ltd. & BAAC

Lighting Consultant Claude & Danielle Engle

Environmental Wind Engineering University of Bristol

Acoustic Consultant ISVR Consultancy Services

Approximate Cost £ 97,500,000

Building Area 85,700 m²

Photography Ken Kirkwood, Richard Davies, Dennis Gilbert

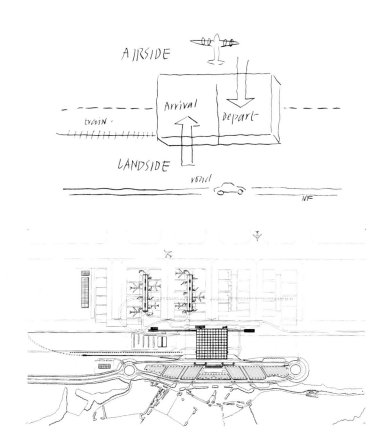

USA

Sir Norman Foster & Partners

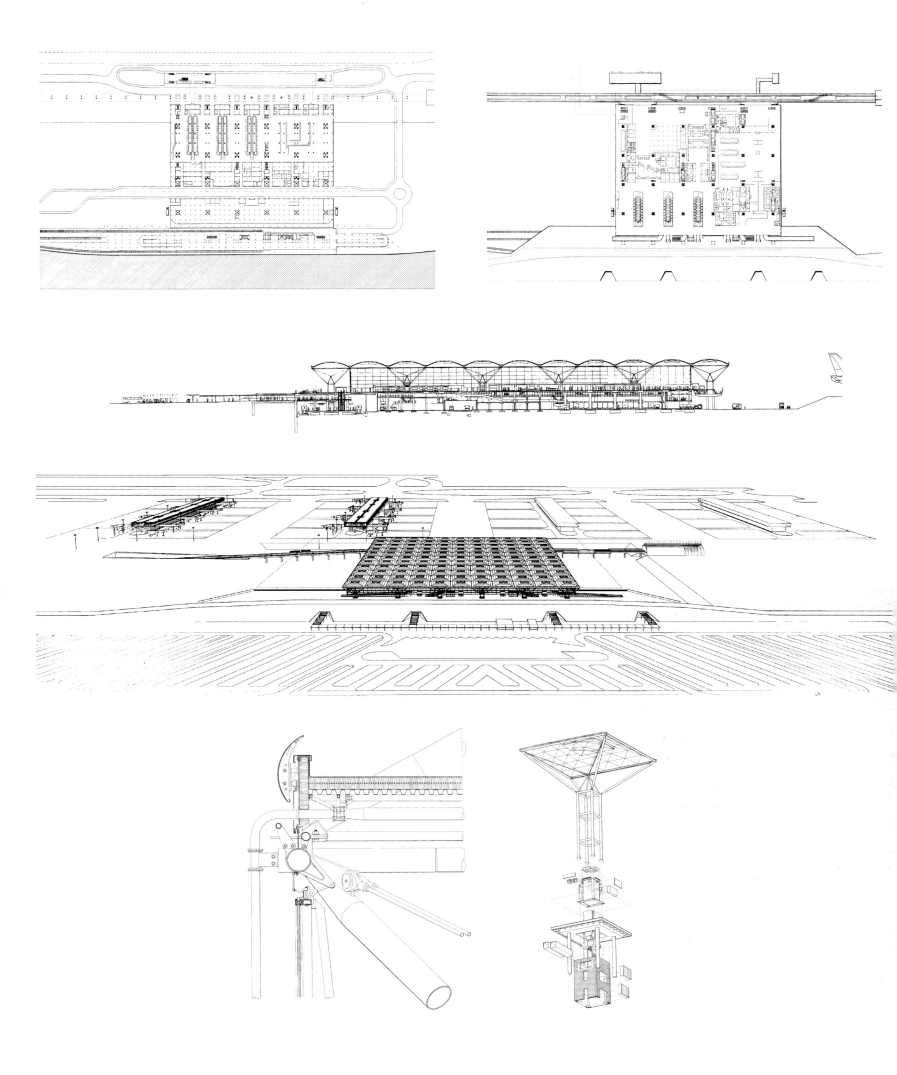

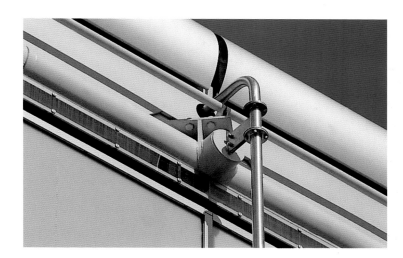

Awards 1- AIA National Honor Award for Architecture / 2- Excellence in Design Award

Given by 1- The American Institute of Architects (AIA); 2- AIA, New York State

Prize Presentation February 1994

Architects Cesar Pelli & Associates, New Haven/Connecticut

Award Winning Building **Carnegie Hall Tower**

Location 152 West 57th Street New York, New York, USA

Design and Construction Period 1987 - 1991

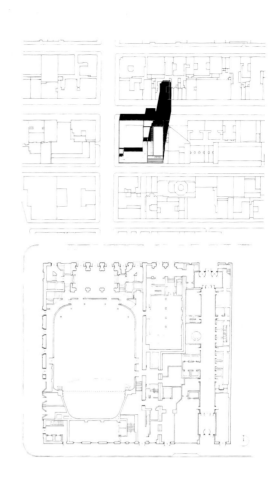

Design Team Cesar Pelli & Associates, New Haven, Connecticut; Design principal: Cesar Pelli; Project Principal: Fred Clarke; Design team leader: Kevin Hart; Project manager: Malcolm Roberts; Designers: Mitchell Hirsch, Robert Bostwick, Mihaly Turbucz, Lisa Winkelmann, Timothy Paxton, Douglas McIntosh; Architect-of-Record: Brennan Beer Gorman, New York; Principal-in-Charge: Frank LaSusa; Project architect: Landis Dooley;

Structural Engineering Robert Rosenwasser Associates, P. C. New York

Mechanical and Electrical Engineering Cosentini Associates, New York

Lighting Mesh & Juul Inc., Greenwich

Site Area 14,000 sq. ft.

Building Area 510,000 sq. ft.

Total Floor Area 14,000 sq. ft.

Photography Jeff Goldberg / Esto and Malcolm Roberts / CP&A

U S A

C e s a r   P e l l i   &   A s s o c i a t e s

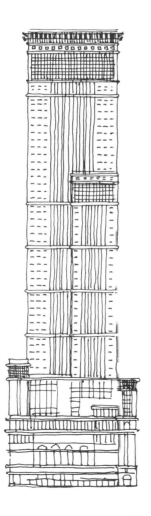
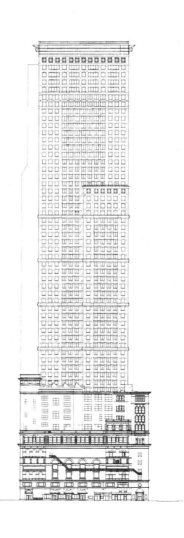
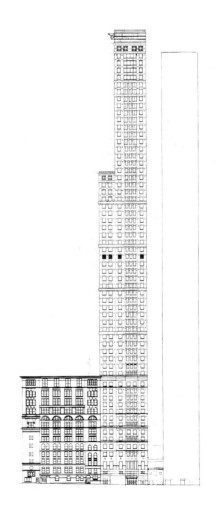

Award AIA National Honor Award for Architecture
Given by The American Institute of Architects
Prize Presentation May / 5 / 1995
Members of the Jury Frances Halsband, Jeanne Giordano,
Suzanne Plucker Irwin, Ralph Johnson, Johnpaul Jones, Mary Oehrlein,
Terrence Sargent
Architects William Rawn Associates, Architects, Inc., Boston
Award Winning Building **Seiji Ozawa Hall at Tanglewood**
Location Lenox, Massachusetts, USA
Design and Construction Period August 1989 - June 1994

Design Team William L. Rawn III (Principal in charge), Alan R. Joslin
(Project architect and manager)
Acoustician R. Lawrence Kierkegaard & Associates
Theatre Consultant Theatre Projects
Lighting Douglas Baker
Structural and Civil Engineering Structural: LeMessurier Consultants;
Civil: Foresight Land Service
Quantity Surveying Donnell Consultants
Landscape Architecture Michael Van Valkenburgh Associates, Inc.
Approximate Cost US$ 9,700,000
Site Area 200 acres
Building Area 36,200 GSF
Photography Steve Rosenthal

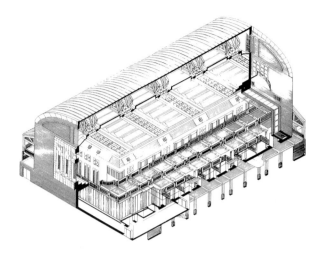

214   **U S A**

W i l l i a m   R a w n   A s s o c i a t e s

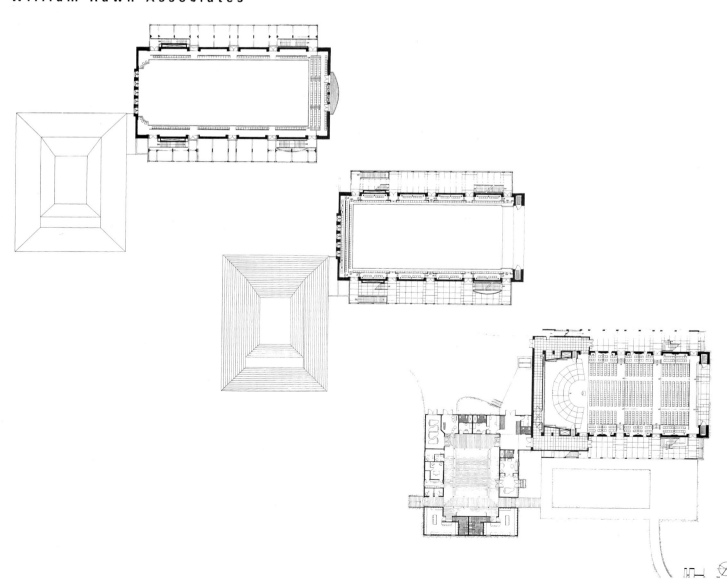

216

USA

217

Award AIA National Honor Award for Architecture
Given by The American Institute of Architects, AIA
Prize Presentation February 1994
Members of the Jury Donlyn Lyndon, Jan Abell, Adele Chatfield-Taylor, Ted Flato, Raymond Gindroz, Peter Van Dijk
Architects Tanner Leddy Maytum Stacy Architects, San Francisco
Award Winning Building **Corson-Heinser Live / Work**
Location San Francisco, California USA
Design and Construction Period 1990 -1992

Structural and Civil Engineering Tannebaum-Manheim Engineers
Site Area 1,500 sq. ft.
Building Area 1,200 sq. ft.
Total Floor Area 4,000 sq. ft.
Photography Thomas Heinser

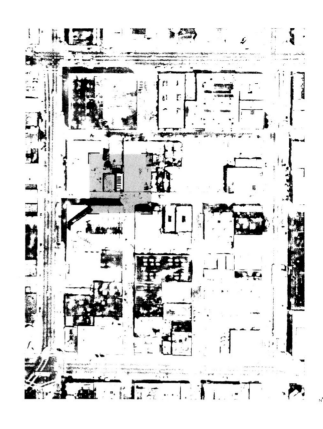

Tanner Leddy Maytum Stacy Architects

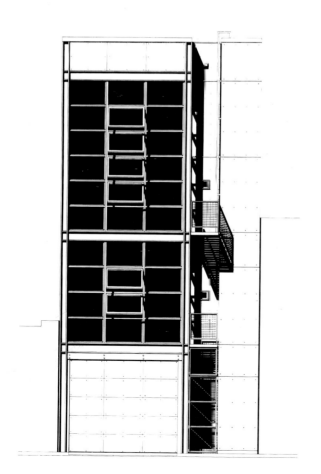

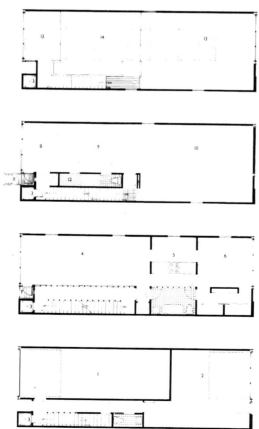

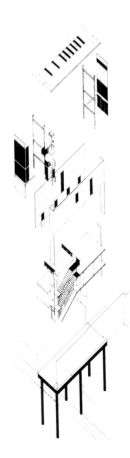

INDEXES

Sections of the UIA (International Union of Architects) and Awards

Algeria
Union des Architectes Algériens, Kouba

Argentina
Federación Argentina de Sociedades de Arquitectos, Buencs Aires

Azerbaijan
Union of Architects of Azerbaijan, Baku

Australia
The Royal Australian Institute of Architects, Canberra
Awards Robin Boyd Award for Housing, International Citation, Commercial Architecture Award, International Award, Environmental Citation, National Interiors Architecture Award, Sir Zelman Cowen Award for Public Buildings, Lachlan Macquarie Award for Conservation, Access Citation, Walter Burley Griffin Award for Urban Design (National Award), Victorian Architecture Medal, Merit Award for Outstanding Architecture - Multiple Residential Category, Merit Award for Civic Design

Austria
Bundeskammer der Architekten und Ingenieurkonsulenten, Wien
Award Staatspreis für Consulting

Baltic States
Association of Unions of Baltic Architects
Esthonia, Latvia, Lithuania, Riga (Latvia)

Bangladesh
Institute of Architects of Bangladesh, Dacca
Award: IAB Gold Medal

Belgium
Fédération Royale des Sociétés d'Architectes de Belgique, Bruxelles (without any Prize Presentation)
Recommendation of the institution: Fondation Philippe Rotthier pour l'architecture

Awards Prix Européen de la Reconstruction de la Ville, Prix Européen de la Reconstruction de la Ville - Category: Espace Public et Projet Urbain

Bolivia
The College of Architects of Bolivia, La Paz

Brazil
Instituto de Arquitectos do Brasil, São Paulo
Awards Prêmio Habitação / Premiação IAB, Annual Award of the Instituto de Arquitectos do Brasil - Departamento de São Paulo - one person residence, Premiação Instituto de Arquitectos do Brasil, Premio Fachada (Best Facade), Premiação IAB / SP - Best Building, Premiação IAB - Category: Edificações-Projeto, Premiação IAB / SP Building for Educational Activities, Premiação IAB / SP Building for Healthcare Services, Premio ex-aequo IAB - Category: Arquitetura de Interiores-Ohra Executada

Bulgaria
Union des Architectes Bulgares, Sofia

Cameroun
Ordre des Architectes du Cameroun, Yaunde

Canada
The Royal Architectural Institute of Canada, Ontario
Award Governor General's Award for Architecture

Central America
Federación Centroamericana de Arquitectos (Costa Rica, Guatemala, Honduras, Nicaragua, El Salvador), Guatemala
Award Mayor de la Ciudad

Chile
Colegio de Arquitectos de Chile, Santiago de Chile

People's Republic of China
The Architectural Society of China, Beijing
Awards Creation Awards of the Architectural Society of China between 1984-1993, Creation Awards of the Architectural Society of China between 1988-1992,

National Excellent Design (Gold Award), World Habitat Awards

Columbia
Sociedad Colombiana de Arquitectos, Bogotá
Award Award of the ›Bienal Colombiana‹

Croatia
Association of Croatian Architects, Zagreb

Cuba
Unión Nacional de Arquitectos e Ingenieros de la Construcción de Cuba, La Habana

Cyprus
The Cyprus Civil Engineers & Architects Association, Nicosia

Czech Republic
Society of Czech Architects, Prague
Award Grand Prix of the Association of Czech Architects

Denmark
Danske Arkitekters Landsforbund, Copenhagen
Awards Den Grønne Nål, The Architectural Prize

Ecuador
Colegio Nacional de Arquitectos del Ecuador, Quito
Awards IX Bienal Panamericana de Arquitectura de Quito - Categoria de Conservacion, Preservacion, Restauracion y Adaptacion a Nuevo Uso del Patrimonio Edificado, IX Bienal Panamericana de Arquitectura de Quito, Mencion de Honor, Architectural Design Grand Award, Gran Premio Internacional IX Bienal Panamericana de Arquitectura de Quito

Egypt
Society of Egyptian Architects, Cairo

Eurasian Group
(Armenia, Bielorussia, Kirgizia, Tadjikistan, Uzbekistan), Moscow
Awards II. Prize and Medal at the International Contest ›Best Architectural Work of 1993‹, Grand Prix of Architecture, Construction and Design

Finland
The Finnish Association of Architects, Helsinki
Award Alvar Aalto Medal

France
Conseil National de l'Ordre des Architectes, Paris (without any Prize Presentation)
Recommendation of the institution: Ministère du Logement, Paris
Awards Equerre d'Argent, Prize for Town Planning, Grand Prix National d'Architecture, Yearly ›Moniteur de l'Architecture‹ Award

Gabun
Ordre des Architectes du Gabon, Libreville

Germany
Bund Deutscher Architekten BDA, Bonn
Award Der Große BDA-Preis

Greece
Chambre Technique de Grèce, Athènes

Hong Kong
The Hong Kong Institute of Architects, Wanchai
Awards Annual Award (President's Prize), ARCASIA Award, HKIA Medal

Hungary
Chamber and Association of Hungarian Architects, Budapest
Awards Pro Architectura Prize, Ybl Miklós Prize

Iceland
Arkitektafelag Islands, Reykjavik

India
The Indian Institute of Architects, Bombay

Indonesia
The Institute of Architects of Indonesia, Jakarta
Awards IAI Award for Architects and their Buildings, IAI Award for Individuals (Architects and Non-Architects) & Institutions

Ireland
The Royal Institute of the Architects of Ireland, Dublin
Awards Award for Architectural Excellence,

RIAI Regional Award
- Dublin
- Northern
- Eastern
- Western
- Southern

Israel
Association of Engineers &
Architects in Israel, Tel Aviv
Awards Zeev Rechter Prize,
Architecture Prize on 1st of July

Italy
Consiglio nazionale degli Architetti,
Roma

Ivory Coast
Conseil national de l'Ordre des
Architectes de Côte d'Ivoire,
Abidjan, Jamaica
The Jamaican Institute of
Architects, Kingston

Japan
Japan Institute of Architects, Tokyo
Awards JIA Prize for the Best
Young Architect of the Year, Annual
Architectural Design
Commendation of the Japan
Institute of Architects, Special
Award for Design Excellence

Kazakhstan
Union of Architects of Kazakhstan,
Alma Ata
Award Le Prix de l'Union des
Architectes de la République du
Kazakhstan

Kenya
The Architectural Association of
Kenya, Nairobi
Award Shilling Award

Korea
The Korean Institute of Architects,
Seoul

Republic of Korea
Union des Architects de la R.P. de
Corée, Pyong-Yang

Kuwait
Kuwait Society of Engineers, Safat

Lebanon
Order of Engineers and Architects,
Beirut

Luxembourg
Ordre des Architectes et des
Ingénieurs du Luxembourg,
Luxembourg
Award Prix Luxembourgeois
d'Architecture

Macau
Associacao dos Arquitectos de
Macau, South East Asia

Macedonia
Association of Architects of the
Former Yougoslavian Republic of
Macedonia, Skopje

Malaysia
Malaysian Institute of Architects,
Kuala Lumpur

Malta
Chamber of Architects and Civil
Engineers, Pembroke
Award Recommendation of
Chamber of Architects and Civil
Engineers of Malta

Mauritius
The Mauritius Association of
Architects MAA, Port Louis

Mexico
Federacion de Colegios de
Arquitectos de la República
Mexicana, Mexico

Mongolia
Union of Mongolian Architects,
Ulan Bator

Morocco
Section Marocaine de l'UIA, Rabat
Award Award of the Ministère de
l'Habitat / ERAC Oriental

Republic of Namibia
Namibia Institute of Architects,
Windhoek
Award Award of Merit: Engraved
Plaque & Certificate of Merit

The Netherlands
Bond van Nederlandse Architekten,
Amsterdam
Awards Grand Prix Rhénan
d'Architecture, National Steel
Award, BNA Kubus, A. J. van
Eyck Prize

Nigeria
The Nigerian Institute of Architects,
Lagos

Norway
Norske Arkitekters Landsforbund,
Oslo
Awards Anton Christian Houens
Fonds Diplom, European Steel
Design Award

Pakistan
Institute of Architects of Pakistan,
Lahore

Panama
Sociedad Panamena de Ingenieros
y Arquitectos, Panama
Awards Best Midsize Apartment
Building of the Year, Best Large
Apartment Building of the Year

Paraguay
Associacion Paraguaya de
Arquitectos, Asunción

Peru
Colegio de Arquitectos del Perú,
Lima
Awards Hexagono de Oro - Bienal
de Arquitectura, Hexagono de Plata
a Mejor Estructura, Hexagono de
Plata a Mejor Uso Materiales

Republic of the Philippines
United Architects of the
Philippines, Metro Manila
Award Likha Award on Gold Medal

Poland
Stowarzyszenie Architektow
Polskich SARP, Warszawa
Awards SARP Honorary Award for
Comprehensive Activities,
Honorary Prize for Comprehensive
Activities

Portugal
Association of Portuguese
Architects, Lisbon
Award Premio Nacional de
Arquitectura

Puerto Rico
Colegio de Arquitectos de Puerto
Rico, Santurce
Award Henri Klumb

Romania
Union of Architects of Romania,
Bucarest
Awards Yearly Award Union of
Romanian Architects, Constantin
Joja, The Major Prize for
Architecture in Romania

Russia
Union of Architects of Russia,
Moscow
Awards First Prize UAR, The State
Prize of the Russian Federation

Senegal
Ordre des Architectes du Senegal,
Dakar

Singapore
Singapore Institute of Architects,
Singapore

Slovakia
Society of Slovakian Architects,
Bratislava
Award Prize of Emil Belluš

Slovenia
Zavod Za Izgradnjo Maribora,
Maribor

Spain
Consejo Superior de los Colegios
de Arquitectos de España, Madrid
Award Diseño Arquitectonico,
Premio Internacional Bienal de
Arquitectura, Medalla de Oro,
Premio de la Bienal de Arquitectura
Española ›Manuela de la Dehesa‹,
Premio Ciutat de Barcelona, Premio
Fad de Arquitectura

Sri Lanka
Sri Lanka Institute of Architects,
Colombo
Award SLIA Design Award

Sweden
Svenska Arkitekters Riksförbund,
SAR, Stockholm
Award SARs Kasper Salin-Pris

Switzerland
1- Association Genevoise
d'Architectes (AGA), Fédération
des Architectes Suisses (FAS),
Société Suisse des Ingénieurs et
des Architectes (SIA)
Award Prix Interassar
2- Hochbauamt Zürich, Büro für
Architektur & Stadtbild, on behalf
of Schweizerischer Ingenieur- und
Architektenverein, SIA, Zürich
Award Auszeichnungen für gute
Bauten in der Stadt Zürich
3- France, Germany, Netherlands,
Switzerland
Award Grand Prix Rhénan
d'Architecture

Syria
Ordre des Ingénieurs et
Architectes Syriens, Damas

Tanzania
The Architectural Association of
Tanzania, Dar-Es-Salam

Thailand
The Association of Siamse
Architects, Bangkok

Trinidad & Tobago
Trinidad & Tobago Institute of
Architects, Port of Spain

Tunisia
Ordre des Architectes de Tunisie,
Cité Mahrajene

Uganda
The Uganda Society of Architects,
Kampala

Ukraine
Union of Architects of Ukraine,
Kiev
Award Award of the Union of
Architects of Ukraine

United Kingdom
The Royal Institute of British
Architects, London
Awards Building of the Year, RIBA
National Award, EAA Building of
the Year,
RIBA Regional Architecture Award
- England, London Region
- England, Northern Region
- England, Southern Region
- England, South East Region
- South West Region
- North West Region
- East Midlands Region
- West Midlands Region
- Scotland
- Wales
- Wessex Region

Uruguay
Sociedad de Arquitectos del
Uruguay, Montevideo
Awards Concurso Obra Realizada
(Periodo 1982-1992), Concurso
Publico de Obra Realizada: Best
Work in the Last 12 Years (1983-
1995)

USA
The American Institute of
Architects, Washington
Awards AIA National Honor Award
for Architecture, Excellence in

Design Award, Design Award, AIA
Gold Medal, AIA Honor Award for
Excellence in Architectural Design,
The AIA Twenty-Five Year Award,
Excellence in Design Award from
AIA New York State

Vietnam (Rep. Dem.)
Union des Architectes du Viet
Nam, Hanoi

Zambia
Zambia Institute of Architects,
Lusaka
Awards Tri-annual Award,
Tri-annual Award in Category of
Commercial

Zimbabwe
Institute of Architects of
Zimbabwe, Harare
Awards Award of Merit, Award
of Excellence, National Award of
Excellence in Architecture -
Certificate of Merit, National
Architecture Award

Architects

Locations

229

© 1996, by Prestel Verlag Munich and New York

Copyright details and photo credits have been submitted by the architects
themselves; neither the Editor nor Prestel Verlag shall be held responsible
for the accuracy of such details.

Prestel books are available worldwide. Please contact your nearest booksel-
ler or write to either of the following addresses for information concerning
your local distributor:

Prestel Verlag, Mandlstrasse 26, D-80802 Munich, Germany
Phone (89) 38 17 09-0, Fax (89) 38 17 09-35

Prestel Verlag, 16 West 22nd Street, New York, N.Y. 10010, USA
Phone (212) 627 81 99, Fax (212) 627 98 66

Die Deutsche Bibliothek – CIP-Einheitsaufnahme
Award Winning Architecture ... : AWA ; international yearbook ...
- Engl. Orig-Ausg. - Munich ; New York : Prestel.
Erscheint jährl. - Aufnahme nach 1996
ISSN 1430-9459
NE: AWA ; international yearbook ...

Design Petra Lüer, Munich
Offset lithography Fischer Repro Technik GmbH, Frankfurt
Printing Pera Druck Matthias KG, Gräfelfing
Binding R. Oldenbourg GmbH, Munich

Printed in Germany
ISBN 3-7913-1676-1
ISSN 1430-9459